P9-CQO-273

1A

Math in Focus®
Singapore Math®
by Marshall Cavendish

Workbook

Consultant and Author
Dr. Fong Ho Kheong

Authors
Chelvi Ramakrishnan and Bernice Lau Pui Wah

U.S. Consultants
Dr. Richard Bisk, Andy Clark, and Patsy F. Kanter

mc Marshall Cavendish
Education

U.S. Distributor

Houghton
Mifflin
Harcourt

COMMON CORE

© Copyright 2009, 2013 Edition Marshall Cavendish International (Singapore) Private Limited
© 2014 Marshall Cavendish Education Pte Ltd

Published by Marshall Cavendish Education
Times Centre, 1 New Industrial Road, Singapore 536196
Customer Service Hotline: (65) 6213 9444
US Office Tel: (1-914) 332 8888 | Fax: (1-914) 332 8882
E-mail: tmesales@mceducation.com
Website: www.mceducation.com

Distributed by
Houghton Mifflin Harcourt
222 Berkeley Street
Boston, MA 02116
Tel: 617-351-5000
Website: www.hmheducation.com/mathinfocus

First published 2009
2013 Edition

All rights reserved. No part of this publication may be reproduced, stored in a retrieval system or transmitted, in any form or by any means, electronic, mechanical, photocopying, recording or otherwise, without the prior permission of Marshall Cavendish Education.

Marshall Cavendish and *Math in Focus®* are registered trademarks of Times Publishing Limited.

Singapore Math® is a trademark of Singapore Math Inc.® and Marshall Cavendish Education Pte Ltd.

Math in Focus® Grade 1 Workbook A
ISBN 978-0-669-01386-3

Printed in Singapore

15 16 17   1401   18
4500696007   A B C D E

Contents

Addition Facts to 10

Subtraction Facts to 10

Shapes and Patterns

Ordinal Numbers and Position

CHAPTER 7

Numbers to 20

CHAPTER 8

Addition and Subtraction Facts to 20

Length

BLANK

Numbers to 10

Practice 1   Counting to 10

Count.
Write the numbers.

Example

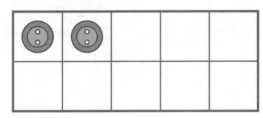

_____
- - - 2 - - -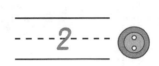
_____

1.

_____
- - - 3 - - - 🐞
_____

2.

_____
- - - 7 - - - 🍐
_____

3.

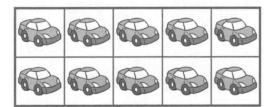

_____
- - 10 - - - 🚗
_____

© Marshall Cavendish International (Singapore) Private Limited.

Count.
Write the numbers.

4.

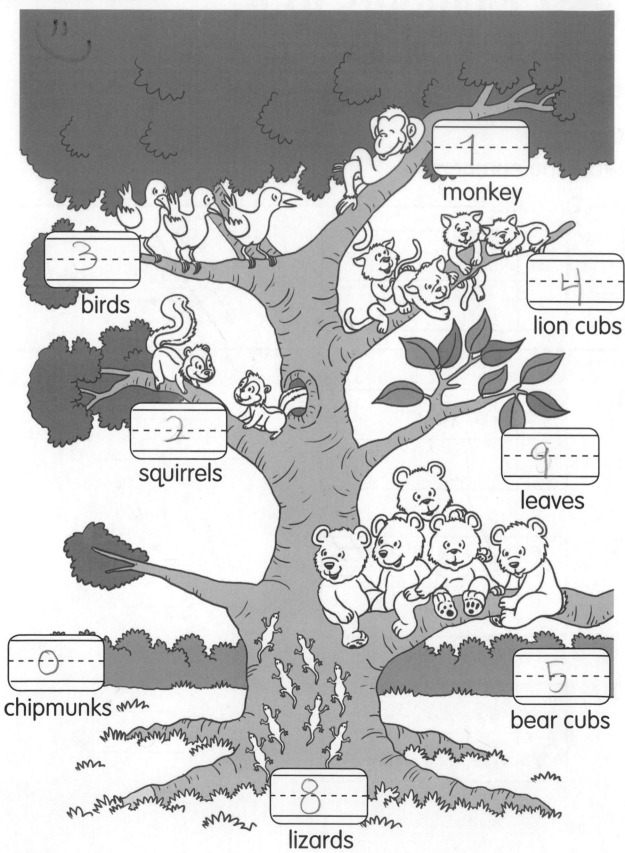

monkey — 1

birds — 3

lion cubs — 4

squirrels — 2

leaves — 9

chipmunks — 0

bear cubs — 5

lizards — 8

© Marshall Cavendish International (Singapore) Private Limited.

Draw.

5. A cow has 2 horns.

6. A chair has 4 legs.

7. An ant has 6 legs.

8. Each ladybug has 10 spots.

© Marshall Cavendish International (Singapore) Private Limited.

How many insects are there?
Match.

9.

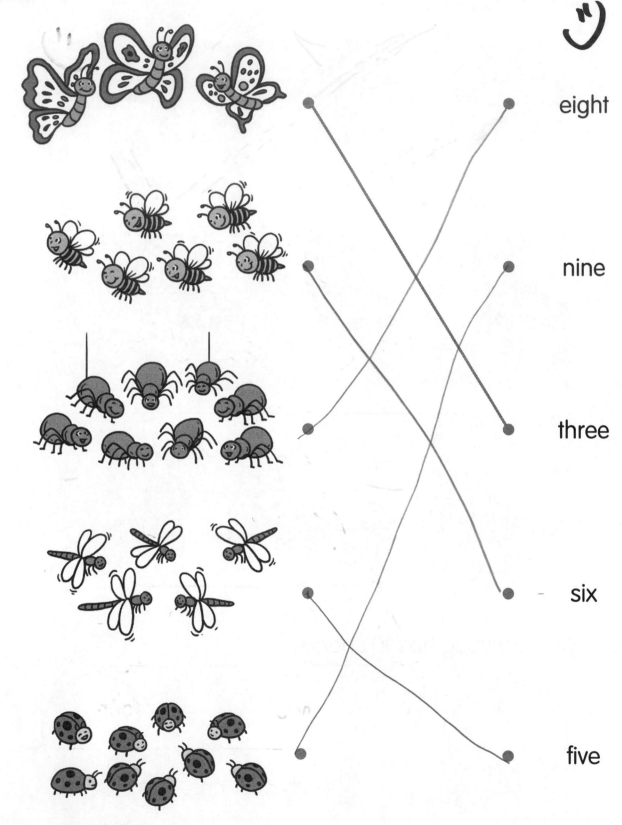

eight

nine

three

six

five

© Marshall Cavendish International (Singapore) Private Limited.

Count the things on the snowman.
Circle the correct words.

10.		(two) three four five (zero)
11.		zero (one) two three four
12.	◯	six seven (eight) nine ten
13.		one two three (four) five
14.		nine six (one) eight three

© Marshall Cavendish International (Singapore) Private Limited.

Match the numbers to the words.

15.

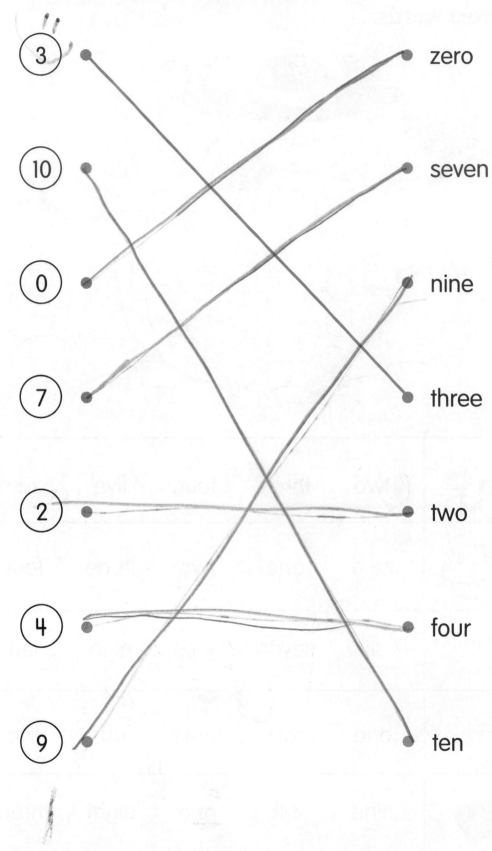

3   zero

10   seven

0   nine

7   three

2   two

4   four

9   ten

© Marshall Cavendish International (Singapore) Private Limited.

Practice 2   Comparing Numbers

Count.
Circle the groups that have the same number.

Example

1.

2.

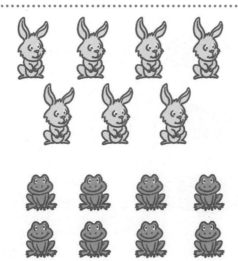

© Marshall Cavendish International (Singapore) Private Limited.

Match. Then circle the answer to each question.

© Marshall Cavendish International (Singapore) Private Limited.

Example

Are there more  than ? (Yes) No

Are there fewer  than ? Yes (No)

Is the number of  and the same? Yes (No)

3.

Are there more than  ? Yes   No

Are there fewer than  ? Yes   No

Is the number of and the same? Yes   No

8   **Chapter 1** Numbers to 10

Match. Then circle the answer.

4.

Are there more than ? Yes No

Are there fewer than ? Yes No

Is the number of  and  the same? Yes No

5.

Are there more than ? Yes No

Are there fewer than ? Yes No

Is the number of  and the same? Yes No

© Marshall Cavendish International (Singapore) Private Limited.

Which two groups have the same number of things?

Join them to a _‒‒‒‒‒‒_.

Then write the number in each _‒‒‒‒‒‒_.

6.

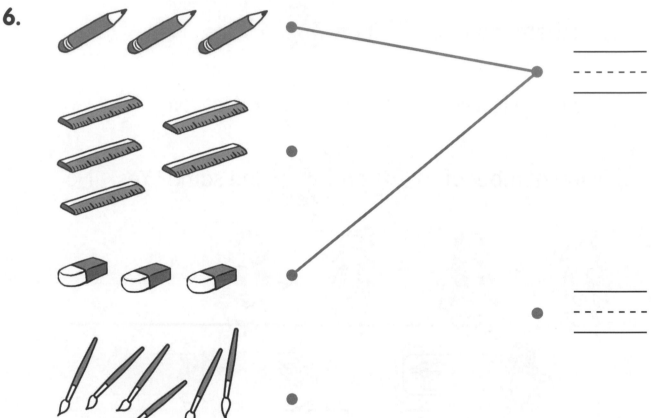

© Marshall Cavendish International (Singapore) Private Limited.

© Marshal Cavendish International (Singapore) Private Limited.

Name: _____ **Date:** _____

Count and write the number.
Then answer each question by coloring the correct box.

Which is more?

Example

--- 4 --- pots 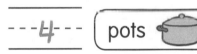   --- 6 --- pears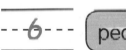

7. _____ cups    _____ teapot

Which is fewer?

8. _____ ladles    _____ muffins

9. _____ gloves   _____ plates

Color the correct signs.

Which number is greater?

10.

11.

Which number is less?

12.

13.

Write the numbers in the blanks.

14.

15.

_____ is greater than _____.   _____ is less than _____.

Color the flags with the same number.

16.

© Marshall Cavendish International (Singapore) Private Limited.

Practice 3   Making Number Patterns

What comes next in each pattern?
Write the number.

1.

_____

2.

_____

3.

_____

What is 1 more?
Write the number.

4.

_____

5.

_____

6.

_____

© Marshall Cavendish International (Singapore) Private Limited.

What is 1 less?
Write the number.

7.

8.

9.

Write the missing numbers in the number patterns.

10.

4   5   8

11.

0   1   4

© Marshall Cavendish International (Singapore) Private Limited.

Write the missing numbers in the number patterns.

12.

13.

14.

15.

© Marshall Cavendish International (Singapore) Private Limited.

Fill in the blanks.

16.　1 more than 1 is _____ .

17.　1 more than 8 is _____ .

18.　1 more than 9 is _____ .

19.　1 less than 7 is _____ .

20.　1 less than 9 is _____ .

21.　1 less than 6 is _____ .

22.　_____ is 1 more than 3.

23.　_____ is 1 more than 6.

24.　_____ is 1 less than 4.

25.　_____ is 1 less than 7.

© Marshall Cavendish International (Singapore) Private Limited.

Put On Your Thinking Cap!

Challenging Practice

Mother Hen's eggs have numbers that are greater than 2 and less than 8.

Color the eggs that belong to Mother Hen.

© Marshall Cavendish International (Singapore) Private Limited.

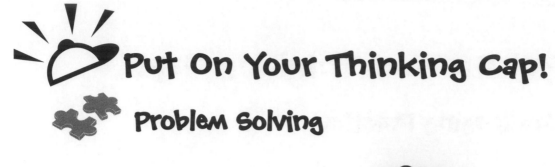

Daryl sees a pattern made with △.

He wants to continue the pattern but does not know

how many △ to draw.

Draw the next group of △ in the box below to continue the pattern.

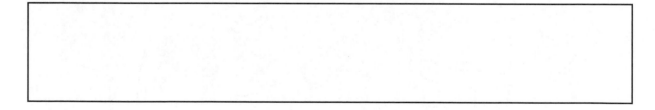

There are _____ △ in the next group.

© Marshall Cavendish International (Singapore) Private Limited.

Chapter Review/Test

Vocabulary

Match.

1. four •——————————————————• 10

2. seven •   • 4

3. ten •   • 7

4. zero •   • 0

Concepts and Skills

Circle the stars to show the number.
Write the number in words.

5. 5 ⭐ ⭐ ⭐ ⭐ ⭐ ⭐ ⭐ ⭐ ⭐ ⭐

_____

6. 9 ⭐ ⭐ ⭐ ⭐ ⭐ ⭐ ⭐ ⭐ ⭐ ⭐

_____

© Marshall Cavendish International (Singapore) Private Limited.

Fill in the blanks with *greater than, less than or the same as*.

cups and saucers   trees   cars

7. The number of cups is _____ the number of saucers.

8. The number of trees is _____ the number of cars.

9. The number of cars is _____ the number of cups.

Write any two numbers.

10. greater than 5: _____ _____.

11. less than 7: _____ _____.

Write the missing numbers in the number pattern.

12.

 6   5   4   1

Fill in the blanks.

13. 4 is 1 less than _____.

14. 9 is 1 more than _____.

© Marshall Cavendish International (Singapore) Private Limited.

Number Bonds

Practice 1 Making Number Bonds

Look at the ▨.
Fill in the parts.

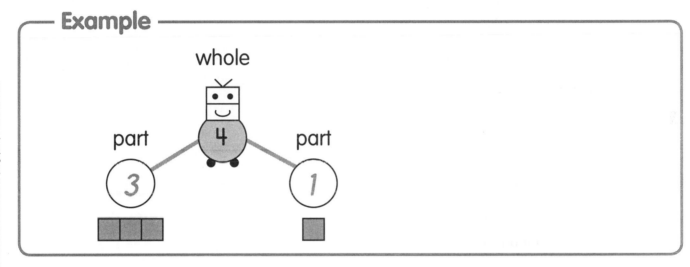

Example

whole

part   part

4

3   1

1.

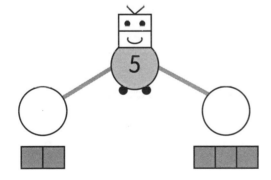

5

2.

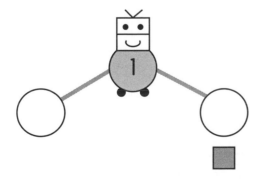

1

© Marshall Cavendish International (Singapore) Private Limited.

Look at the ▦.
Fill in the whole.

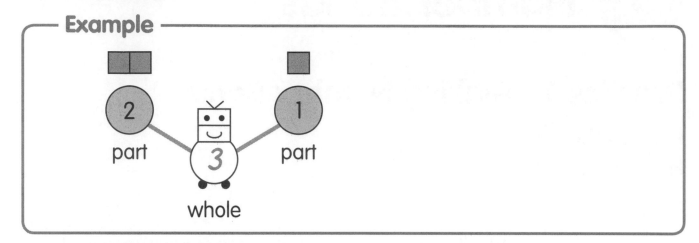

Example

part   whole   part

3.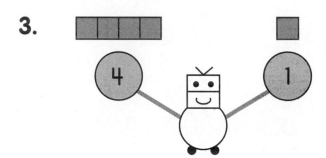

4.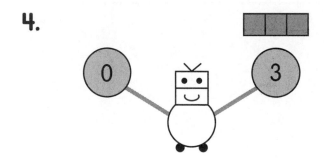

5.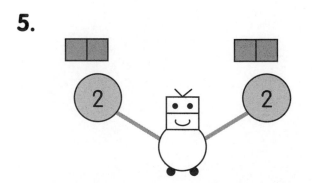

© Marshall Cavendish International (Singapore) Private Limited.

Look at the ▮.
Fill in the parts.

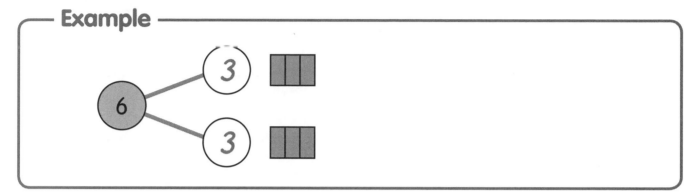

Example

6 — 3 ▮▮▮
   — 3 ▮▮▮

6.

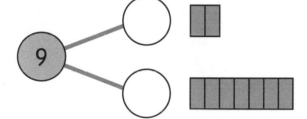

9 — ○ ▮▮
  — ○ ▮▮▮▮▮▮▮

7.

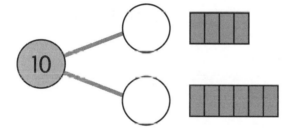

10 — ○ ▮▮▮▮
   — ○ ▮▮▮▮▮▮

8.

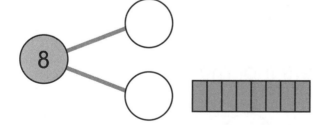

8 — ○
  — ○ ▮▮▮▮▮▮

9.

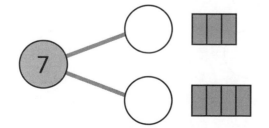

7 — ○ ▮▮▮
  — ○ ▮▮▮▮

© Marshal Cavendish International (Singapore) Private Limited.

Complete the number bonds.
Fill in the blanks.

10. What numbers make 10?

── **Example** ───────────────────────

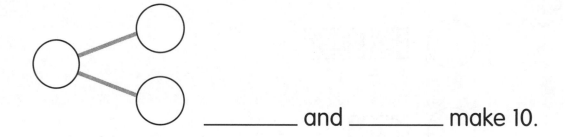

_____4_____ and _____6_____ make 10.

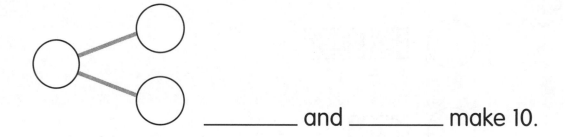

_____ and _____ make 10.

_____ and _____ make 10.

11. Are there any other numbers that make 10?

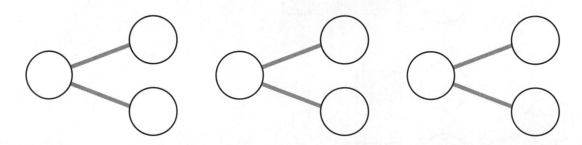

© Marshall Cavendish International (Singapore) Private Limited.

Name: _____ Date: _____

Practice 2   Making Number Bonds

Look at the pictures.
Complete the number bonds.

Example

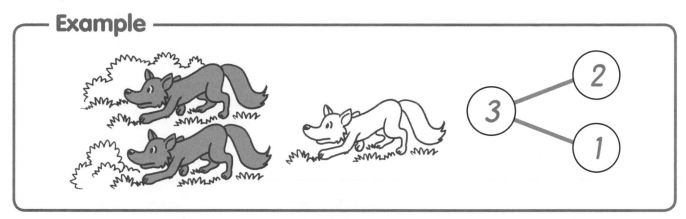

1.

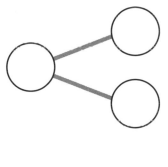

2.

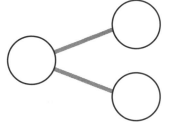

© Marshall Cavendish International (Singapore) Private Limited.

Look at the pictures.
Complete the number bonds.

3.

  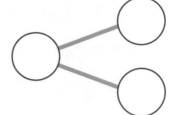

4.

  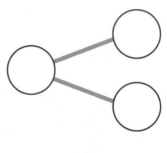

5.

  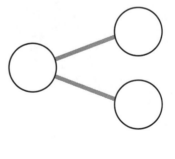

6.

  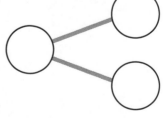

© Marshall Cavendish International (Singapore) Private Limited.

Practice 3   Making Number Bonds

Match to make 8.

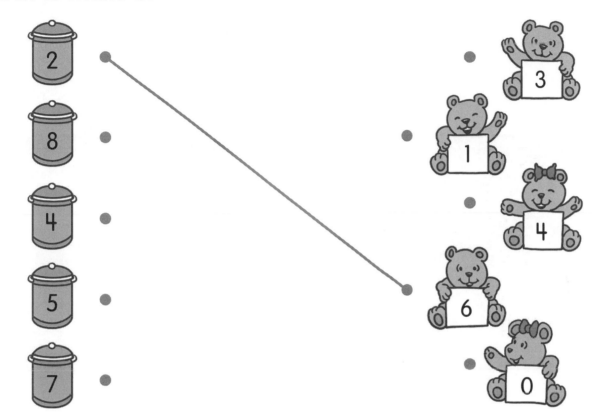

1.

Match the numbers.

2. Match to make 6.

0
4
5
3

3
1
6
2

3. Match to make 9.

8
2
3
4

6
5
1
7

© Marshall Cavendish International (Singapore) Private Limited.

Look at the picture.
Complete the number bonds.

4.

Look at the number bond.
Draw the correct number of butterflies.

5.

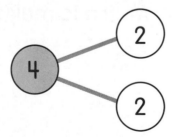

© Marshall Cavendish International (Singapore) Private Limited.

Use two colors. Color the ☐ to show two numbers that make the number in ◯.
Complete the number bonds.
Fill in the blanks.

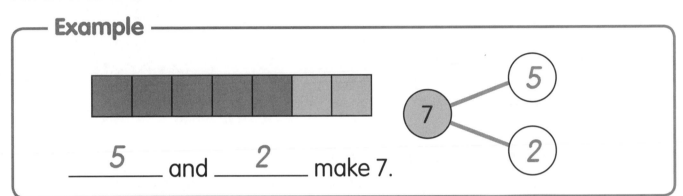

Example

_____5_____ and _____2_____ make 7.

6.

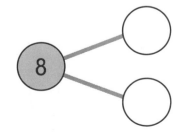

_____ and _____ make 10.

7.

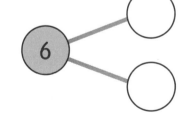

_____ and _____ make 6.

8.

_____ and _____ make 8.

© Marshall Cavendish International (Singapore) Private Limited.

Use two colors.
Color the ☐ **to show two numbers that make 5.**
Complete the number bonds.
Fill in the blanks.

9.

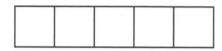

_____ and _____ make 5.

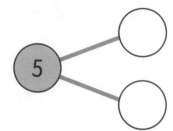

10.

_____ and _____ make 5.

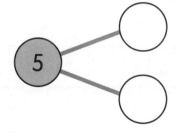

11.

_____ and _____ make 5.

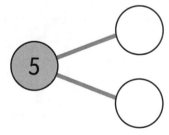

© Marshall Cavendish International (Singapore) Private Limited.

Put On Your Thinking Cap!

Challenging Practice

Make a number bond with three numbers from the bag.
Use each number once.

1.

2.

© Marshall Cavendish International (Singapore) Private Limited.

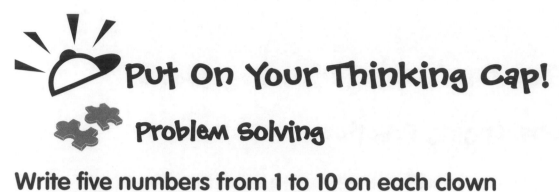 Put On Your Thinking Cap!

Problem Solving

Write five numbers from 1 to 10 on each clown
to complete the number bonds.
Use each number once for each clown.

Example

1.

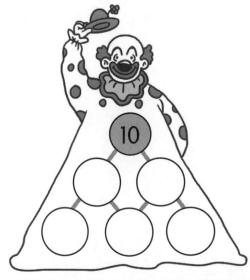

2.

© Marshall Cavendish International (Singapore) Private Limited.

© Marshall Cavendish International (Singapore) Private Limited.

Name: _____   Date: _____

Chapter Review/Test

Vocabulary

Choose the correct word.

1.

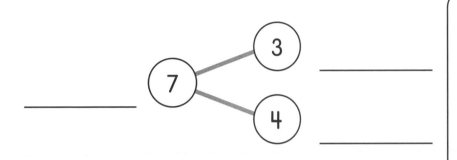

_____

number bond
part
whole
part

_____

_____

2.   3, 4, and 7 make a _____.

Concepts and Skills

Complete the number bonds.
Fill in the blanks.

3.

      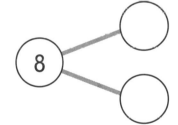

_____

_____

_____ and _____ make 8 insects.

What numbers make 7?

4.

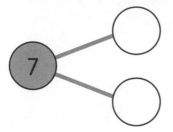 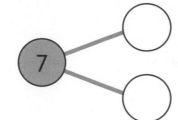 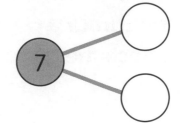

Look at the picture.
Complete the number bond.
Fill in the blanks.

5.

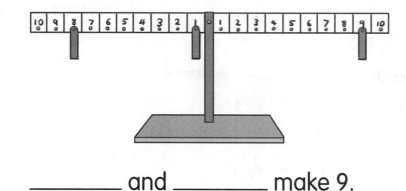 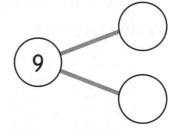

_____ and _____ make 9.

What other numbers make 9?

6.

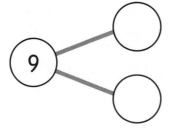 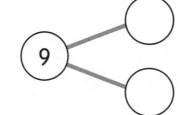 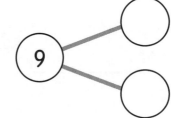

© Marshall Cavendish International (Singapore) Private Limited.

Cumulative Review

for Chapters 1 and 2

Concepts and Skills

Count.
Write the numbers.

1.

There are _____ .

2.

There are _____ .

3.

There are _____ 🔵 .

© Marshall Cavendish International (Singapore) Private Limited.

Match the numbers to the words.

4.

 1 •

 5 •

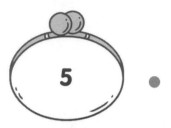 0 •

 8 •

 9 •

 6 •

• eight

• nine

• one

• five

• zero

• six

© Marshall Cavendish International (Singapore) Private Limited.

Name: _____ Date: _____

Circle the group that has <u>more</u>.

5.

Circle the group that has <u>fewer</u>.

6.

Circle the groups that have the <u>same</u> number.

7.

© Marshall Cavendish International (Singapore) Private Limited.

Color the fish with the number that is <u>less</u>.

8.

9.

Color the fish with the number that is <u>greater</u>.

10.

11.

Complete the number patterns.

12.

13.

Fill in the blanks.

14. 1 more than 5 is _____.

15. _____ is 1 less than 7.

© Marshall Cavendish International (Singapore) Private Limited.

© Marshall Cavendish International (Singapore) Private Limited.

Name: _____   Date: _____

Count and complete each number bond.
Then fill in the blanks.

16.

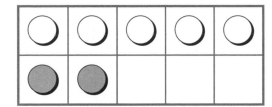

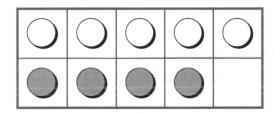

_____ and _____ make 7.

17.

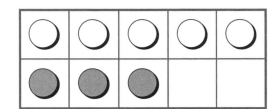

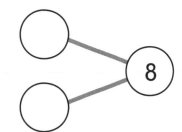

_____ and _____ make 8.

18.

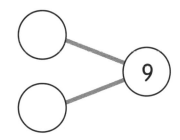

_____ and _____ make 9.

19.

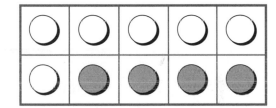

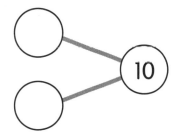

_____ and _____ make 10.

Write the missing numbers.
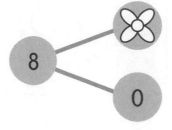 stands for a number.

20.

 is _____.

21.

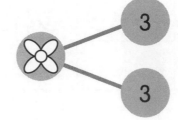

 is _____.

22.

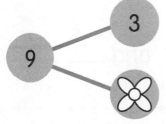

 is _____.

23.

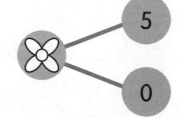

 is _____.

© Marshall Cavendish International (Singapore) Private Limited.

CHAPTER 3 Addition Facts to 10

Practice 1 Ways to Add

Add. Count on from the greater number.

Example

$4 +$ __3__ $=$ __7__

1.

$6 +$ _____ $=$ _____

2.

$5 +$ _____ $=$ _____

3.

$7 +$ _____ $=$ _____

4.

$8 +$ _____ $=$ _____

© Marshall Cavendish International (Singapore) Private Limited.

Look at the pictures.
Add. Count on from the greater number.

Example

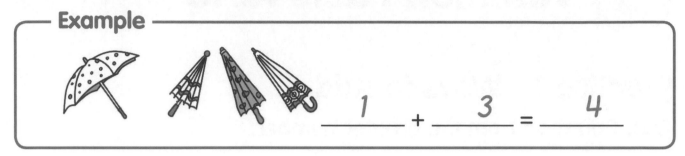

_____1_____ + _____3_____ = _____4_____

5.

_____ + _____ = _____

6.

_____ + _____ = _____

7.

_____ + _____ = _____

8.

_____ + _____ = _____

© Marshall Cavendish International (Singapore) Private Limited.

Count on to add.

9.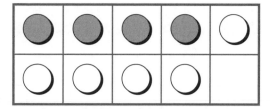

_____ + _____ = _____

10.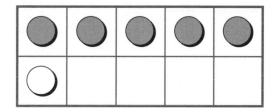

_____ + _____ = _____

11.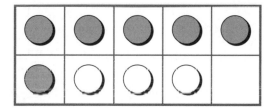

_____ + 1 = _____

12.

_____ + _____ = _____

© Marshal Cavendish International (Singapore) Private Limited.

Count on from the greater number to add.

13. 4 + 1 = _____   **14.** 6 + 2 = _____

15. 9 + 1 = _____   **16.** 3 + 4 = _____

17. 3 + 7 = _____   **18.** 4 + 5 = _____

Complete.
Write the answer in each ☐.

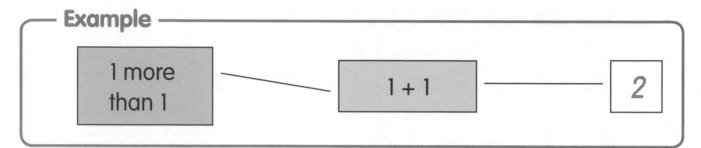

Example

| 1 more than 1 | — | 1 + 1 | — | 2 |

19.

| 2 more than 6 | — | 6 + 2 | — | ☐ |

20.

| 4 more than 5 | — | 5 + 4 | — | ☐ |

21.

| 3 more than 7 | — | 7 + 3 | — | ☐ |

22.

| 2 more than 8 | — | 8 + 2 | — | ☐ |

© Marshall Cavendish International (Singapore) Private Limited.

Practice 2   Ways to Add

Complete the number bonds.

Then fill in the blanks.

┌─ **Example** ──┐

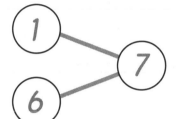   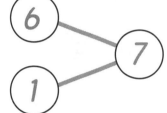

$\underline{1} + \underline{6} = \underline{7}$ $\underline{6} + \underline{1} = \underline{7}$

$\underline{1} + \underline{6} = \underline{6} + \underline{1}$

└──┘

1.

   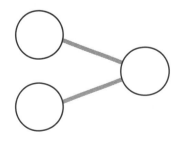

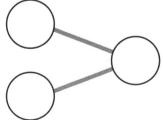

_____ + _____ = _____   _____ + _____ = _____

_____ + _____ = _____ + _____

© Marshall Cavendish International (Singapore) Private Limited.

2.

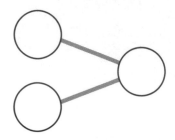 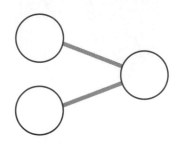

_____ + _____ = _____   _____ + _____ = _____

_____ + _____ = _____ + _____

3.

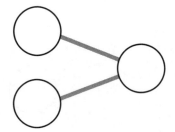 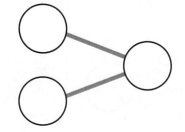

_____ + _____ = _____   _____ + _____ = _____

_____ + _____ = _____ + _____

© Marshall Cavendish International (Singapore) Private Limited.

© Marshall Cavendish International (Singapore) Private Limited.

Complete the number bonds.
Then fill in the blanks.

4. 1 + _____ = 5

5. 4 + _____ = 5

6. _____ + 5 = 8

7. _____ + 3 = 8

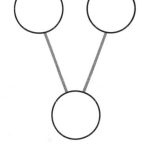

8. 10 + _____ = 10

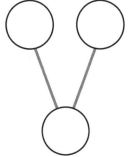

9. _____ + 10 = 10

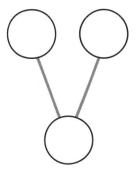

Help each Momma Butterfly find her babies!
Color the small butterflies that match her number.

10.   $1+4$  $4+1$  $3+3$

11.   $2+7$  $3+5$  $5+3$

12.   $7+0$  $0+7$  $3+5$

13.  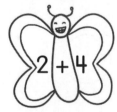 $2+4$  $3+2$  $5+1$

14.   $2+6$  $1+8$  $4+5$

© Marshall Cavendish International (Singapore) Private Limited.

Add.
You can draw number bonds to help you.

15.

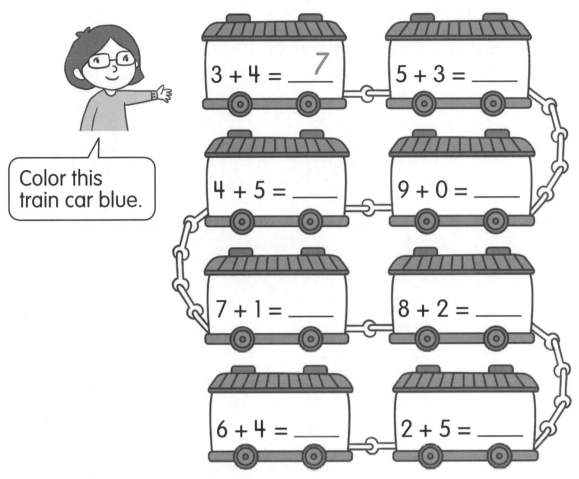

Color this train car blue.

$3 + 4 = \underline{7}$

$5 + 3 = \underline{}$

$4 + 5 = \underline{}$

$9 + 0 = \underline{}$

$7 + 1 = \underline{}$

$8 + 2 = \underline{}$

$6 + 4 = \underline{}$

$2 + 5 = \underline{}$

© Marshall Cavendish International (Singapore) Private Limited.

Now color the train cars above.
Then fill in the table with your answers.

16.

If your answer is	Color	Number of train cars
7	blue	
8	green	
9	orange	
10	red	

Solve.

17. A ball falls into the number machine.
Which ball is it?
Write the correct number on the ball below.

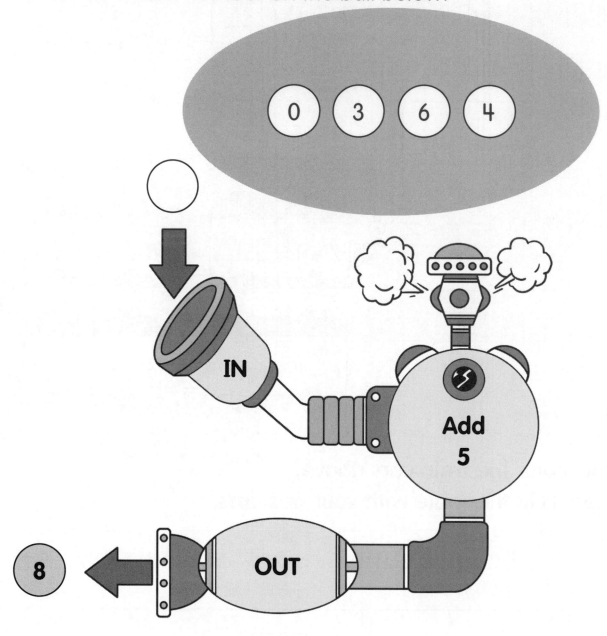

Practice 3   Making Addition Stories

Use the pictures to make addition stories.
Use number bonds to help you.

Example

__4__ 🐘 are playing.

__2__ 🐘 join them.

$$\boxed{4} \;\oplus\; \boxed{2} \;=\; \boxed{6}$$

There are __6__ 🐘 in all.

1.

There are _____ 🦭 .

There are _____ 🦭 .

☐ ◯ ☐ ◯ ☐

There are _____  in all.

© Marshall Cavendish International (Singapore) Private Limited.

2.

_____ are clapping.

_____ are resting.

☐ ◯ ☐ ◯ ☐

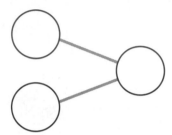

There are _____ in all.

3.

_____ are in a race.

_____ join them.

☐ ◯ ☐ ◯ ☐

_____ runners are in the race now.

© Marshall Cavendish International (Singapore) Private Limited.

4.

Sonia has _____ .

She buys _____ .

Sonia has _____ in all.

5.

There are _____ .

There are _____ .

There are _____ in all.

© Marshall Cavendish International (Singapore) Private Limited.

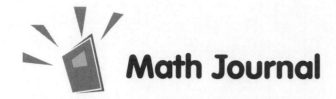

Math Journal

Write your own addition story.

Use the helping words.

Before you begin, color each group of pencils a different color.

pencils	buys	new	pencils	in all

_____

_____

_____

_____

□ ○ □ ○ □

_____

© Marshall Cavendish International (Singapore) Private Limited.

Practice 4   Real-World Problems: Addition

Solve.
Write addition sentences to help you.

Example

____2____ girls are reading.

____1____ boy joins them.

How many children are reading now?

$$2 + 1 = 3$$

____3____ children are reading now.

1.

There are _____ bells.

Beavy brings _____ more bells.

How many bells are there now?

There are _____ bells now.

© Marshall Cavendish International (Singapore) Private Limited.

2.

This toy has _____ straight legs.

It has _____ curly legs.

How many legs does the toy have in all?

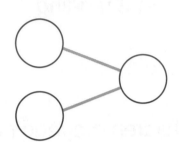

The toy has _____ legs in all.

3.

Mariah has _____ apples.

She has _____ oranges.

How many fruits does Mariah have in all?

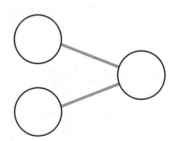

Mariah has _____ fruits in all.

© Marshall Cavendish International (Singapore) Private Limited.

© Marshall Cavendish International (Singapore) Private Limited.

Put On Your Thinking Cap!

 ## Challenging Practice

Solve.

Ivy and Reena have 10 prizes in all.
They do not have the same number of prizes.
How many prizes can Reena have?

There is more than one correct answer!

Reena can have _____ prizes.

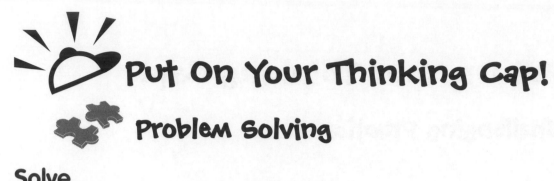

Put On Your Thinking Cap!

Problem Solving

Solve.

Lilian has these candles.
Help her choose the correct number candle for her
friend's birthday.

- Cross out two numbers that add up to 5.
- Cross out two numbers that add up to 10.
- Look at the two numbers that are left.
  Cross out the number that is the least.

The correct number candle is _____.

© 2009 Marshall Cavendish International (Singapore) Private Limited

Chapter Review/Test

Vocabulary

Choose the correct word.

plus	
add	
equal to	
more than	
addition sentence	

1. You can _____ by counting on from the greater number.

2. 2 + 3 = 5 is an _____.

3. 3 plus 4 is _____ 7.

4. "+" is read as _____.

5. 6 is 2 _____ 4.

Concepts and Skills

Add by counting on from the greater number.

6. 3 + 6 = _____   7. 7 + 1 = _____

8. 2 + 8 = _____   9. 1 + 9 = _____

Fill in the blanks.

10. _____ is 3 more than 6.

11. _____ is 2 more than 5.

12. _____ is 4 more than 4.

© Marshall Cavendish International (Singapore) Private Limited.

Look at the pictures.
Fill in the blanks.

13.

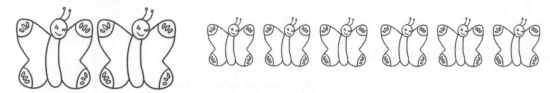

There are _____ big 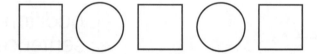.

There are _____ small .

There are _____ in all.

Complete the number bonds.
Fill in the blanks.

14.

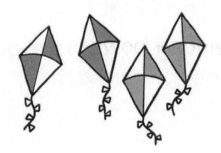

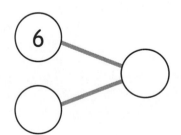

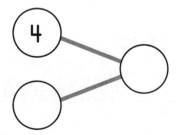

6 + _____ = _____

4 + _____ = _____

6 + 4 = 4 + _____

© Marshall Cavendish International (Singapore) Private Limited.

Name: _____ Date: _____

Problem Solving

Solve.

15. Carlos has 3 brown belts.
He has 2 black belts.
How many belts does he have in all?

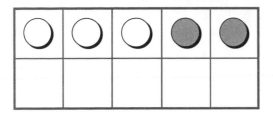

$3 + 2 =$ _____

Carlos has _____ belts in all.

16. Jane has 4 bows.
She gets 3 more bows.
How many bows does she have now?

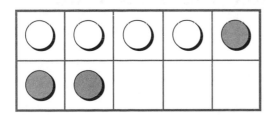

$4 + 3 =$ _____

Jane has _____ bows now.

**Draw .
Then solve.**

17. How many toys are there in all?

3 + _____ = _____

There are _____ toys in all.

Look at the ⊞ **in question 17 to answer the
questions.**

Circle the correct answer.

18. **a.** Are there more or more ?

There are more  .

b. How many more?

5 is [3] [2] more than 3.

© Marshall Cavendish International (Singapore) Private Limited.

Subtraction Facts to 10

CHAPTER 4

Practice 1   Ways To Subtract

Cross out to subtract.

Then circle the answer.

Example

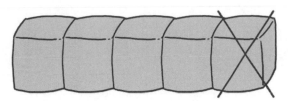

$5 - 1 = ?$ 3   ④   5

1.

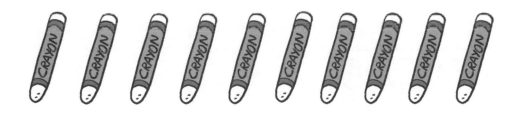

$10 - 1 = ?$ 9   8   7

2.

$8 - 2 = ?$ 2   6   8

© Marshall Cavendish International (Singapore) Private Limited.

Write a subtraction sentence for each picture.

© Marshall Cavendish International (Singapore) Private Limited.

Example

9 – ___1___ = ___8___

3.

5 – _____ = _____

4.

9 – _____ = _____

5.

10 – _____ = _____

6.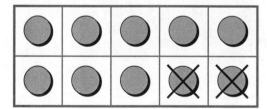

6 – _____ = _____

Complete.

Example

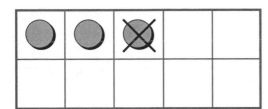

What is 1 less than 3?

$3 - 1 =$ ____2____

7.

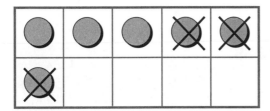

What is 3 less than 6?

$6 - 3 =$ _____

Cross out to subtract.
Then write the subtraction sentence.

Example

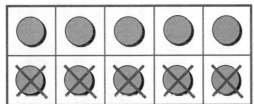

What is 5 less than 10?

10 (-) 5 (=) 5

8. What is 4 less than 7?

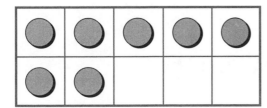   

© Marshall Cavendish International (Singapore) Private Limited.

Cross out to subtract.
Then write the subtraction sentence.

9. What is 2 less than 9?

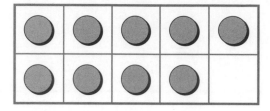

□ ○ □ ○ □

Subtract.
Count on from the number that is less.
Fill in the blanks.

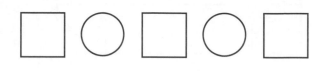

Example

$5 - 2 = \underline{\quad 3 \quad}$

Start here

| 1 | **2** | 3 | 4 | **5** |

1 2 **3**

Count on 3 steps

10. $7 - 4 = \underline{\qquad}$

| 1 | 2 | 3 | 4 | 5 | 6 | 7 |

11. $5 - 3 = \underline{\qquad}$

| 1 | 2 | 3 | 4 | 5 |

12. $8 - 4 = \underline{\qquad}$

| 1 | 2 | 3 | 4 | 5 | 6 | 7 | 8 |

© Marshall Cavendish International (Singapore) Private Limited.

Count back from the greater number to subtract. Fill in the blanks.

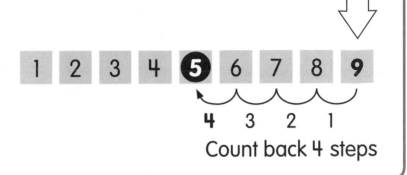

Example

$9 - 4 =$ _____5_____

Start here ⬇

1 2 3 4 **5** 6 7 8 **9**

4 3 2 1

Count back 4 steps

---

13. $10 - 1 =$ _____

1 2 3 4 5 6 7 8 9 10

14. $8 - 2 =$ _____

1 2 3 4 5 6 7 8

15. $7 - 3 =$ _____

1 2 3 4 5 6 7

16. $5 - 4 =$ _____

1 2 3 4 5

17. $8 - 5 =$ _____

1 2 3 4 5 6 7 8

18. $6 - 4 =$ _____

1 2 3 4 5 6

© Marshall Cavendish International (Singapore) Private Limited.

Color the correct shape.

© Marshall Cavendish International (Singapore) Private Limited.

Example

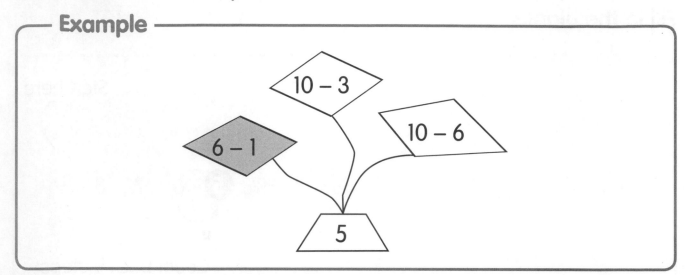

19.

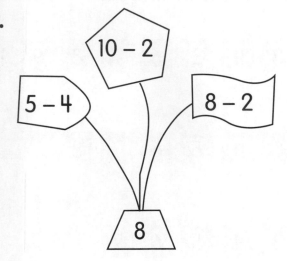

20.

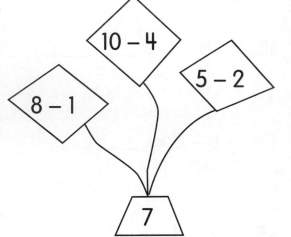

21.

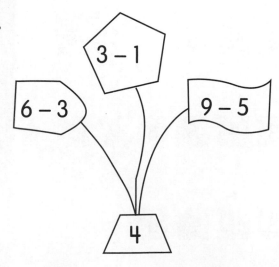

22.

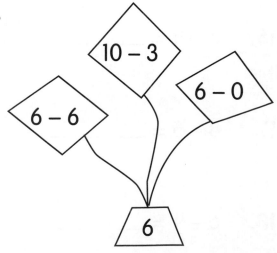

© Marshall Cavendish International (Singapore) Private Limited.

Practice 2   Ways To Subtract

Fill in each number bond.
Then complete the subtraction sentence.

Example

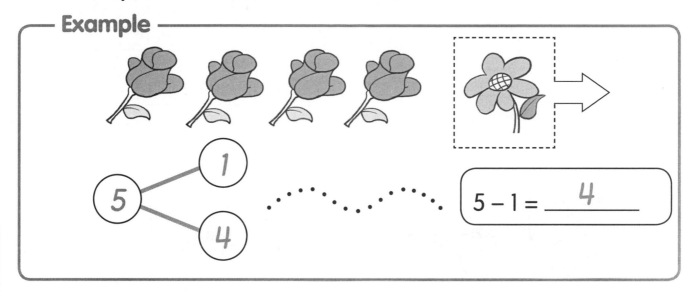

5 – 1 = ___4___

1.

6 – 3 = _____

2.

7 – 4 = _____

3.

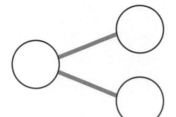 . . . . $8 - 3 = \underline{\hspace{2cm}}$

4.

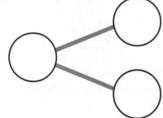 . . . . $9 - 3 = \underline{\hspace{2cm}}$

5.

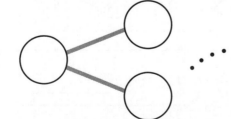 . . . . $10 - 8 = \underline{\hspace{2cm}}$

© Marshall Cavendish International (Singapore) Private Limited.

Name: _____ Date: _____

Fill in the number bonds.
Then write the missing numbers in the subtraction sentences.

Example

$7 - 1 =$ _____6_____

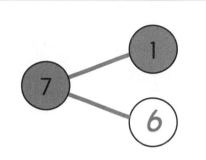

---

6. $10 - 3 =$ _____

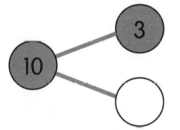

7. _____ $- 1 = 9$

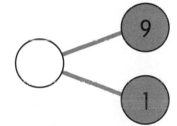

8. $4 -$ _____ $= 4$

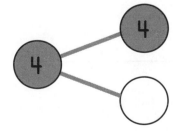

9. _____ $- 5 = 4$

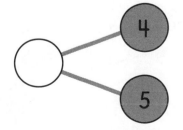

© Marshall Cavendish International (Singapore) Private Limited.

Some stickers are torn off.
Write a subtraction sentence to find how many are left.

© Marshall Cavendish International (Singapore) Private Limited.

Example

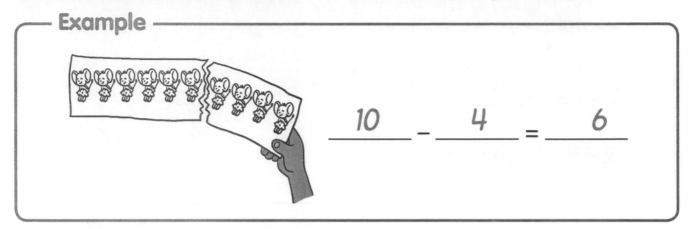

$$\underline{\quad 10 \quad} - \underline{\quad 4 \quad} = \underline{\quad 6 \quad}$$

10.

$$\underline{\qquad} - \underline{\qquad} = \underline{\qquad}$$

11.

$$\underline{\qquad} - \underline{\qquad} = \underline{\qquad}$$

12.

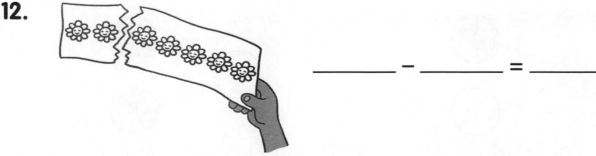

$$\underline{\qquad} - \underline{\qquad} = \underline{\qquad}$$

© Marshall Cavendish International (Singapore) Private Limited.

Name: _____ **Date:** _____

Subtract.
Then match the answers to show where each animal lives.

13.

┌─ **Example** ─┐

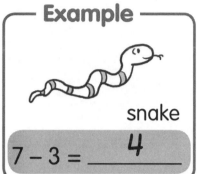
snake

$7 - 3 = \underline{4}$

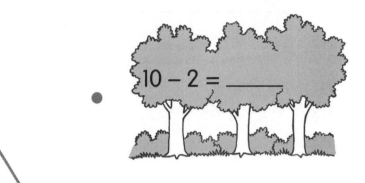

$10 - 2 = \underline{\hspace{1.5cm}}$

kitten

$10 - 5 = \underline{\hspace{1.5cm}}$

$8 - 4 = \underline{4}$

beaver

$8 - 2 = \underline{\hspace{1.5cm}}$

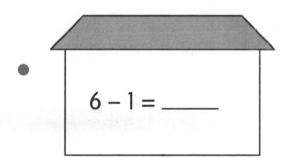

$6 - 1 = \underline{\hspace{1.5cm}}$

squirrel

$9 - 1 = \underline{\hspace{1.5cm}}$

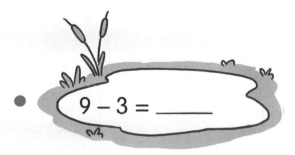

$9 - 3 = \underline{\hspace{1.5cm}}$

Complete.
Then write the letters in the correct ☐ **to solve the riddle.**

14. $10 - 5 =$ _____ 5 **R**

15. $9 - 8 =$ _____ **I**

16. $6 - 3 =$ _____ **B**

17. $7 - 5 =$ _____ **S**

18. $9 - 4 =$ _____ **R**

19. $10 - 0 =$ _____ **A**

20. $9 - 1 =$ _____ **E**

21. $6 - 2 =$ _____ **V**

22. $10 - 3 =$ _____ **K**

23. $9 - 0 =$ _____ **N**

Where do fish keep their money?

In | R | | | | | | | | | |
5   1   4   8   5   3   10   9   7   2

© Marshall Cavendish International (Singapore) Private Limited.

Practice 3   Making Subtraction Stories

Look at the pictures.
Make subtraction stories.
Write subtraction sentences for each story.

Example

There are ___8___ pumpkins.

Jesse takes ___2___ pumpkins away.

[8] (-) [2] (=) [6]

___6___ pumpkins are left.

8 → 2, 6

1.

There are _____ children.

_____ children wear glasses.

[ ] ( ) [ ] ( ) [ ]

_____ children do not wear glasses.

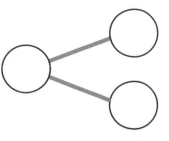

2.

There are _____ mice.

All the mice run away.

_____ mice are left.

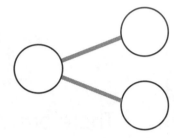

3.

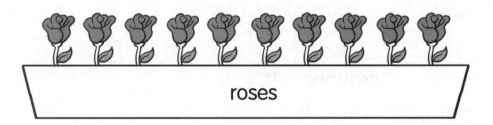

roses

tulips

There are _____ flowers.

_____ flowers are tulips.

_____ flowers are roses.

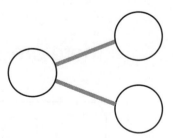

© Marshall Cavendish International (Singapore) Private Limited.

4.

Lola has _____ crayons.

She gives _____ crayons to Pete.

□ ○ □ ○ □

Lola has _____ crayons left.

© Marshall Cavendish International (Singapore) Private Limited.

Math Journal

Color some bunnies brown.
Then make a subtraction sentence.

1. Sally has 9 bunnies.

    _____ bunnies are brown.

    How many bunnies are white?

    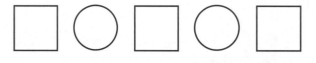

    _____ bunnies are white.

Draw some balls in the drawer.
Cross some out.
Then make a subtraction sentence.

2. Jane has _____ balls.

    Her dog chews _____ of the balls.

    How many balls does she have left?

    Jane has _____ balls left.

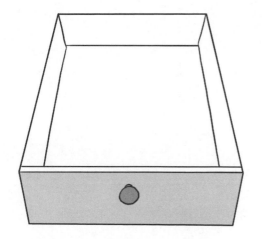

© Marshall Cavendish International (Singapore) Private Limited.

Practice 4   Real-World Problems: Subtraction

Solve.

Example

There are 5 people.
1 person walks away.
How many people are left?

$$5 - 1 = 4$$

There are ____4____ people left.

1.

Kate has 7 buttons.
None of them are white.
How many black buttons are there?

There are _____ black buttons.

2.

8 crabs are on the beach.
2 crabs crawl away.
How many crabs are left?

_____ crabs are left.

© Marshal Cavendish International (Singapore) Private Limited.

Solve.

3.

Brian has 9 toys.
6 of them are cars and the rest are bears.
How many bears does Brian have?

Brian has _____ bears.

4.

There are 10 eggs in a basket.
3 eggs roll out.
How many eggs are left?

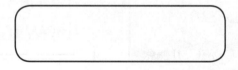

_____ eggs are left.

5.

Abby blows 4 soap bubbles.
She pops all of them.
How many bubbles are left?

_____ bubbles are left.

© Marshall Cavendish International (Singapore) Private Limited.

Practice 5   Making Fact Families

Write a fact family for each picture.

Example

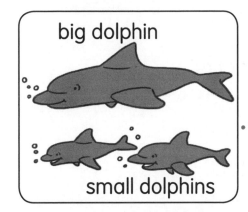

big dolphin

small dolphins

$$\underline{1} + \underline{2} = \underline{3}$$
$$\underline{2} + \underline{1} = \underline{3}$$
$$\underline{3} - \underline{1} = \underline{2}$$
$$\underline{3} - \underline{2} = \underline{1}$$

1.

_____ + _____ = _____

_____ + _____ = _____

_____ − _____ = _____

_____ − _____ = _____

2.

_____ + _____ = _____

_____ + _____ = _____

_____ − _____ = _____

_____ − _____ = _____

© Marshall Cavendish International (Singapore) Private Limited.

Solve.
Use related facts to help you.

3.   Simone has some tomatoes.
       She throws away 5 rotten tomatoes.
       She has 4 tomatoes left.
       How many tomatoes did she have at first?

       ☐ − 5 = 4

       5 + 4 = ☐ is the related addition fact.

       She had _____ tomatoes at first.

4.   Marcus has 6 magnets.
       Susan gives him some magnets.
       Marcus now has 9 magnets.
       How many magnets did Susan give Marcus?

       6 + ☐ = 9

       9 − 6 = ☐ is the related subtraction fact.

       Susan gave Marcus _____ magnets.

Find the missing number.
Use related facts to help you.

5.   ☐ + 5 = 10   6.   2 + ☐ = 7

7.   ☐ − 8 = 2   8.   9 − ☐ = 3

© Marshall Cavendish International (Singapore) Private Limited.

© Marshall Cavendish International (Singapore) Private Limited.

Name: _____   Date: _____

  # Put On Your Thinking Cap!

Challenging Practice

Pick three numbers to make a fact family.
Then write each fact family.

1.

2.

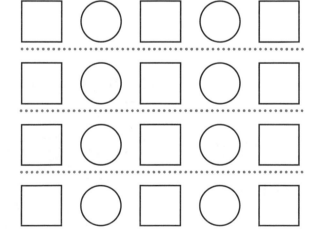

 # Put On Your Thinking Cap!

 ## Problem Solving

Read this riddle.

--- **Example** ---

I think of two numbers.
When I add the numbers, the answer is 5.

$$0 + 5 = 5$$
$$1 + 4 = 5$$
$$2 + 3 = 5$$

When I subtract the numbers, the answer is 1.

$$5 - 0 = 5 \quad ✗$$
$$4 - 1 = 3 \quad ✗$$
$$3 - 2 = 1 \quad ✓$$

What are the two numbers?
The two numbers are 2 and 3.

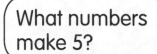

What numbers make 5?

Now you try.

I think of two numbers.
When I add the numbers, the answer is 8.

When I subtract the numbers, the answer is less than 6.

What can the two numbers be?

The two numbers can be _____ and _____.

There is more than one correct answer.

© Marshall Cavendish International (Singapore) Private Limited.

Chapter Review/Test

Vocabulary

Choose the correct word.

1.   + is plus, – is _____.

2.   3 is _____ 7.

3.   8 – 2 means to _____ 2 from 8.

4.   4 – 3 = 1 is a _____.

> subtraction
> sentence
> _____
> take away
> _____
> minus
> _____
> less than

Concepts and Skills

Complete each subtraction sentence.

5.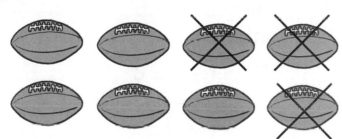

      8 – _____ = _____

6.   What is 4 less than 6?

      6 – _____ = _____

© Marshall Cavendish International (Singapore) Private Limited.

7. What is 3 less than 9?

9 – _____ = _____

Count on from the number which is less.

8. 6 – 3 = _____

9. 9 – 7 = _____

Count back from the greater number.

10. 10 – 5 = _____

11. 7 – 6 = _____

Complete the number bond.
Then complete the subtraction sentence.

12. 7 – 2 = ?

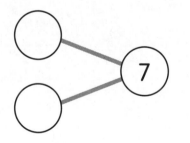

7 – 2 = _____

13. ? – 2 = 8

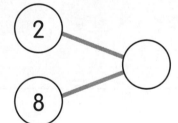

_____ – 2 = 8

Subtract.
Use related facts.

14. 8 – 4 = _____

15. 7 – 3 = _____

16. 10 – _____ = 7

17. 5 – _____ = 5

© Marshall Cavendish International (Singapore) Private Limited.

Write a subtraction story.

18.

_____

_____

_____

_____ – _____ = _____

_____

Write a fact family.

19.

_____ + _____ = _____

_____ + _____ = _____

_____ – _____ = _____

_____ – _____ = _____

© Marshall Cavendish International (Singapore) Private Limited.

Problem Solving

Draw .
Cross them out to solve.
Then write a number sentence.

20.   James has 9 fish in his fish tank.
      He gives his friend 4 fish.
      How many fish does he have left?

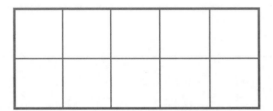

_____ – _____ = _____

James has _____ fish left.

Solve.
Use related facts to help you.

21.   Mr. Peterson bakes 10 pies.
      He eats some of them.
      He now has 8 pies.
      How many pies did he eat?

10 – _____ = 8

Mr. Peterson ate _____ pies.

© Marshall Cavendish International (Singapore) Private Limited.

Cumulative Review

for Chapters 3 and 4

Concepts and Skills

Look at the pictures.
Complete the number sentences.

1.

```
[      ] + [      ] = [      ]
```

2.

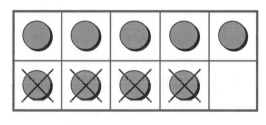

```
[      ] − [      ] = [      ]
```

Complete the number bonds.
Fill in the blanks.

3.   _____ + 5 = 10

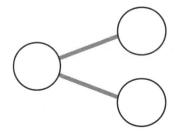

4.   8 − 3 = _____

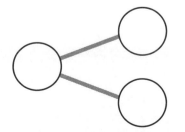

© Marshall Cavendish International (Singapore) Private Limited.

Fill in the blanks.

5. 2 more than 8 is _____.

6. 3 less than 7 is _____.

7. _____ is 2 more than 5.

8. _____ is 5 less than 10.

Find the missing number.
Use related facts to help you.

9. 2 + _____ = 8

10. _____ − 6 = 0

Pick three numbers and make a fact family.

11.

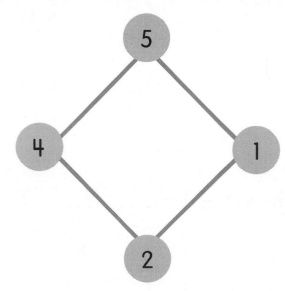

© Marshall Cavendish International (Singapore) Private Limited.

© Marshall Cavendish International (Singapore) Private Limited.

Problem Solving
Look at the pictures.
Write an addition or subtraction story.

12.

There are _____ .

There are _____ .

□ ○ □ ○ □

There are _____ in all.

13.

There are _____ .

Jamal lets go of _____ .

□ ○ □ ○ □

_____ are left.

Solve.
Write addition or subtraction sentences.

14. Ellen has 3 spoons.
Her sister gives her 5 spoons.
How many spoons does Ellen have now?

Ellen has _____ spoons now.

15. There are 8 fish in a fish tank.
6 are angelfish and the rest are goldfish.
How many goldfish are there?

There are _____ goldfish.

© Marshall Cavendish International (Singapore) Private Limited.

© Marshall Cavendish International (Singapore) Private Limited.

Name: _____ Date: _____

CHAPTER
5 **Shapes and Patterns**

Practice 1   Exploring Plane Shapes

Trace the dots.
Then match each shape to its name.

1.

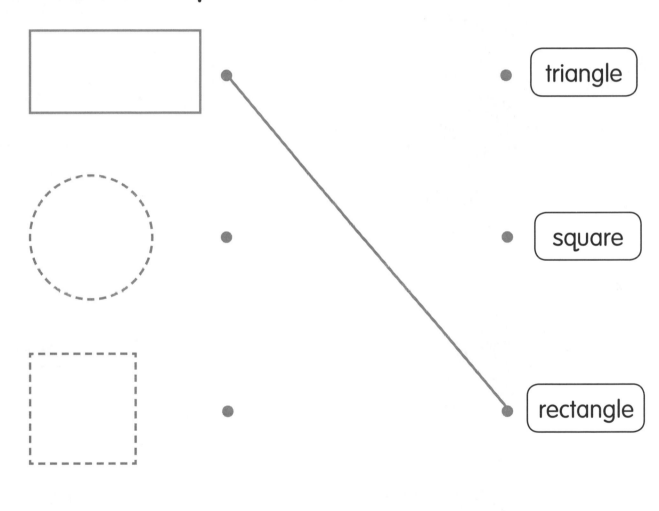

triangle

square

rectangle

circle

A part of each shape is missing.
Think about what shape it was.
Then match the shape to its name.

2.

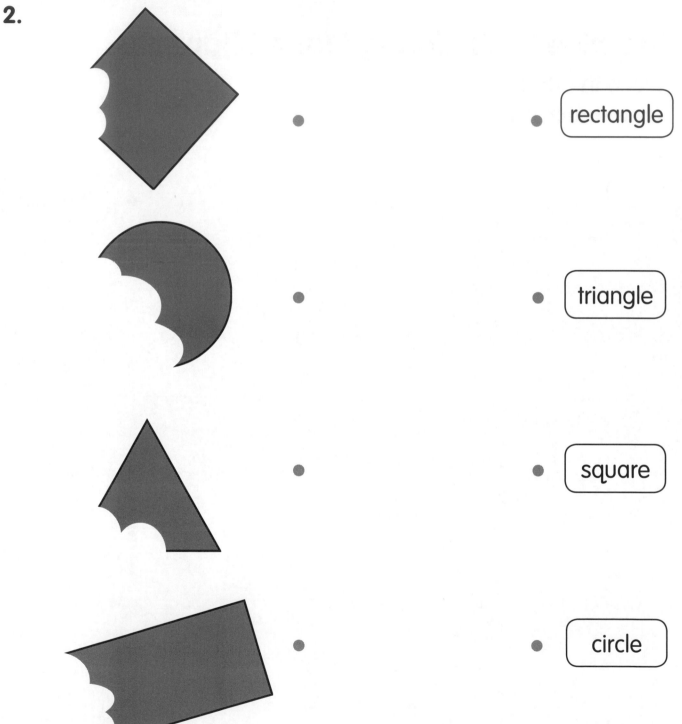

rectangle

triangle

square

circle

© Marshall Cavendish International (Singapore) Private Limited.

© Marshal Cavendish International (Singapore) Private Limited.

Name: _____   **Date:** _____

Circle the shapes that are the same shape as the shaded shape.

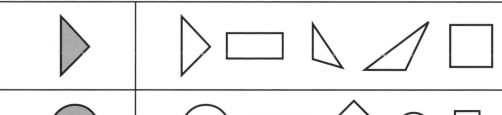

Color the shapes.

7.   squares

8.   triangles

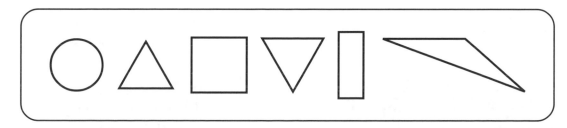

Color the shapes.

9. rectangles

10. The shapes that are <u>not</u> circles.

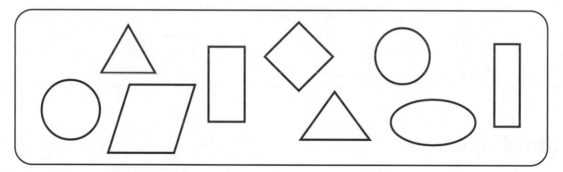

Which shape is <u>not</u> in each set?
Circle the correct answer.

11.

Set A

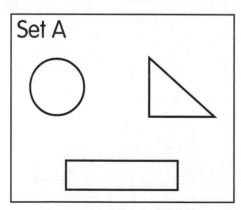

A rectangle/square is not in this set.

12.

Set B

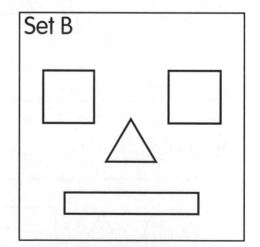

A triangle/circle is not in this set.

© Marshall Cavendish International (Singapore) Private Limited.

© Marshall Cavendish International (Singapore) Private Limited.

Name: _____   **Date:** _____

How many sides and corners are there?
Count.

13.

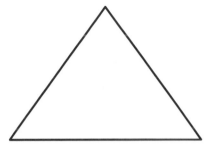

_____ sides

_____ corners

14.

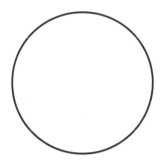

_____ sides

_____ corners

Sort the shapes by <u>color</u>.
Circle the shape that is <u>different</u>.

15.

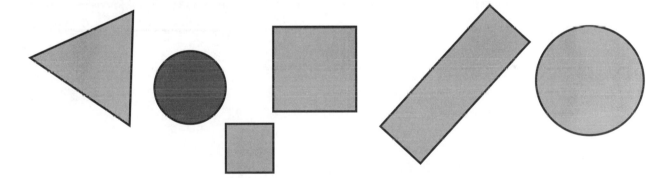

Sort the shapes by <u>size</u>.
Color the shapes that are <u>alike</u>.

16.

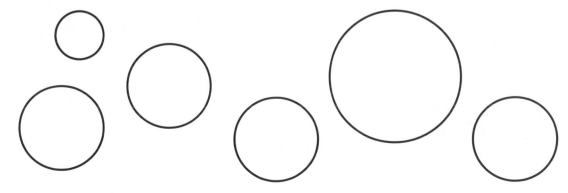

Sort the shapes by <u>shape</u>.
Color the shapes that are <u>alike</u>.

17.

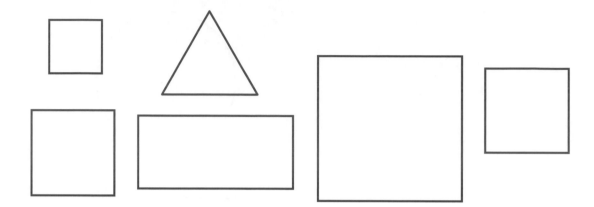

Sort the shapes by <u>corners</u>.
Circle the shape that is <u>different</u>.

18.

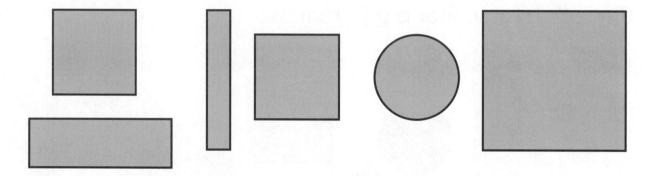

Sort the shapes by the <u>number of sides</u>.
Circle the shape that is <u>different</u>.

19.

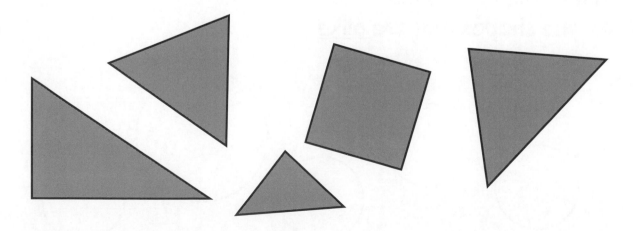

© Marshall Cavendish International (Singapore) Private Limited.

Practice 2   Exploring Plane Shapes

Read.

Then answer the questions.

1.   Josh has a square piece of paper.
     He folds it and unfolds it.
     Then he draws a line along the fold.
     Now he has two new shapes, A and B.

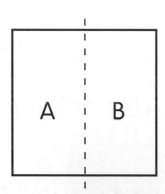

Write *yes* or *no*.

   a.   Are Shape A and Shape B the same shape? _____

   b.   Are Shape A and Shape B the same size? _____

Count.

   c.   How many sides are there?

          Shape A _____   Shape B _____

   d.   How many corners are there?

          Shape A _____   Shape B _____

© Marshall Cavendish International (Singapore) Private Limited.

Write *yes* or *no*.

    e.   Are Shape A and Shape B <u>different</u>? _____

Josh then cuts out Shape A and Shape B.

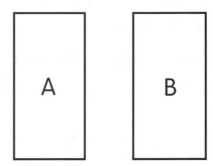

    f.   Can Shape A fit exactly over Shape B? _____

Are the shapes the <u>same</u> shape and size?
Write *yes* or *no*.

2.

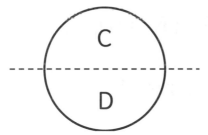

                                Shapes C and D _____

3.

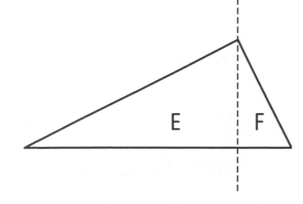

                                Shapes E and F _____

Practice 3   Exploring Solid Shapes

Match each shape to its name.

1.

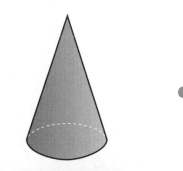
   •   •   cube

   •   •   cone

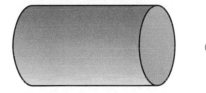
   •   •   pyramid

   •   •   sphere

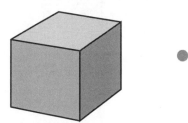
   •   •   cylinder

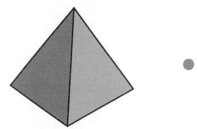
   •   •   rectangular prism

© Marshall Cavendish International (Singapore) Private Limited.

Answer the questions.
Circle the shapes.

2. Which shapes are <u>not</u> cylinders?

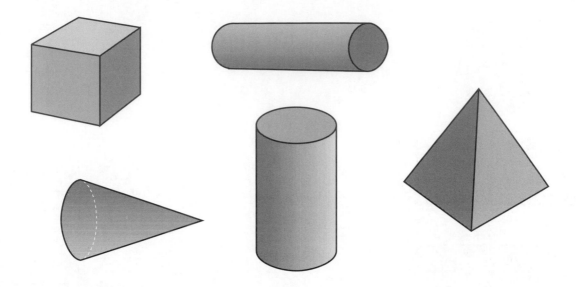

3. Which shapes are <u>not</u> pyramids?

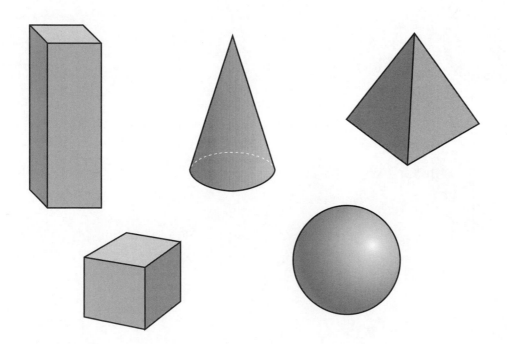

© Marshall Cavendish International (Singapore) Private Limited.

Answer the questions.
Circle the shapes.

4.   Which shapes can you stack?

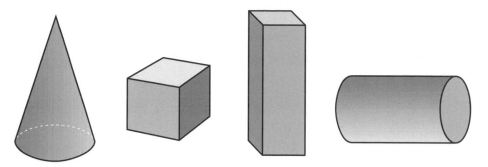

5.   Which shapes can you slide?

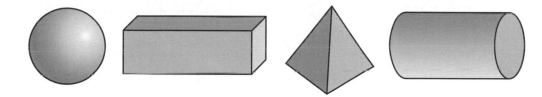

6.   Which shapes can you roll?

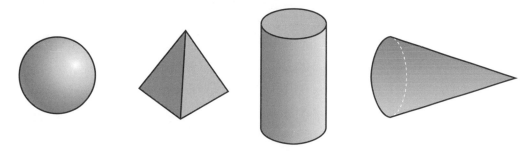

© Marshall Cavendish International (Singapore) Private Limited.

7. Which shape can you <u>only</u> slide?

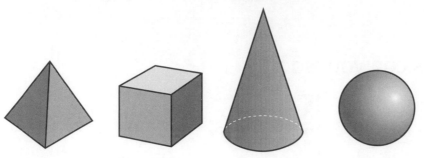

8. Which shape can you <u>only</u> roll?

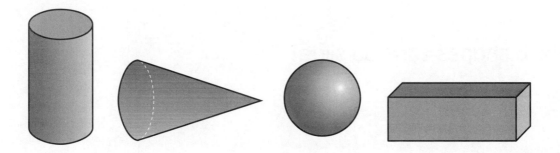

© Marshall Cavendish International (Singapore) Private Limited.

Practice 4   Making Pictures and Models with Shapes

Find the shapes in the pictures.
Count how many of each shape there are.
Write the number.

© Marshall Cavendish International (Singapore) Private Limited.

1.

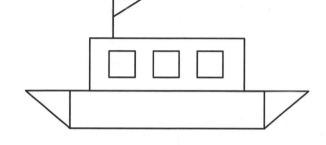

Shape		Number
△	triangle	3
○	circle	
▭	rectangle	
☐	square	

2.

Shape		Number
△	triangle	
○	circle	
▭	rectangle	
☐	square	

Match the pieces to make a shape.
Name the shapes.
Use the words in the box.

circle
square
triangle
rectangle

3.

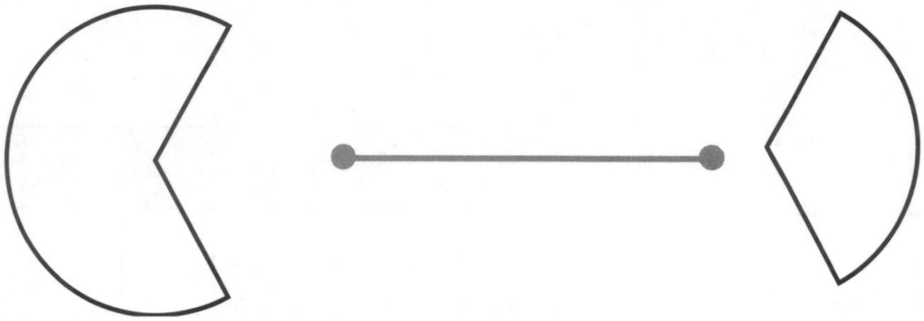

circle

4.

5.

6.

© Marshall Cavendish International (Singapore) Private Limited.

Cut out the shapes below and make a picture.
Paste the picture here or use your own paper.
You do not need to use all the shapes.

7.

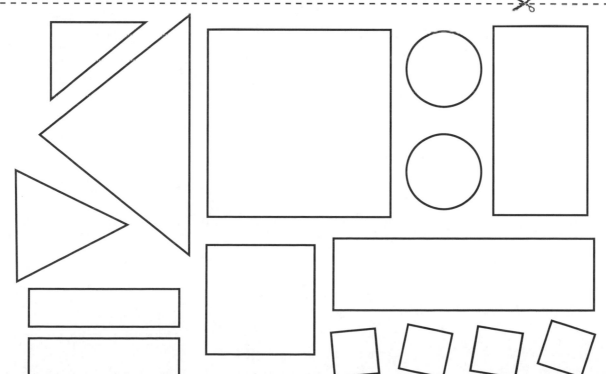

© Marshall Cavendish International (Singapore) Private Limited.

BLANK

Look at the pictures.
Then fill in the blanks.

8. How many triangles can you see?

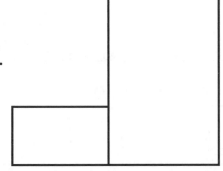

I can see _____ triangles.

9. A star can be made of triangles.

This star is made of _____ triangles.

Draw triangles another way to make up this star.

This star is made of _____ triangles.

© Marshall Cavendish International (Singapore) Private Limited.

10. **Draw a picture with shapes.**
    Count how many of each shape there are.
    Write the number.

Shape		Number
△	triangle	
◯	circle	
▭	rectangle	
▢	square	

© Marshall Cavendish International (Singapore) Private Limited.

Practice 5 Making Pictures and Models with Shapes

Look at the pictures.
Count how many of each solid shape there are.
Write the number.

1.

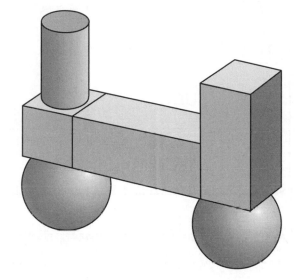

	Shape	Number
	sphere	
	cylinder	
	rectangular prism	
	cone	
	cube	
	pyramid	

© Marshall Cavendish International (Singapore) Private Limited.

2.

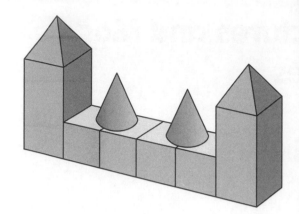

Shape		Number
●	sphere	
▮	cylinder	
▱	rectangular prism	
△	cone	
◻	cube	
◭	pyramid	

3.

Shape		Number
●	sphere	
▮	cylinder	
▱	rectangular prism	
△	cone	
◻	cube	
◭	pyramid	

© Marshall Cavendish International (Singapore) Private Limited.

Name: _____ Date: _____

Practice 6   Seeing Shapes Around Us

Trace the shape of each thing.
Then color.

1.

● Circles - red	■ Squares - yellow	
▲ Triangles - blue	▬ Rectangles - green	

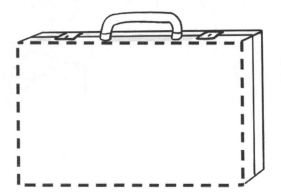
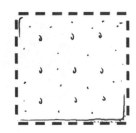

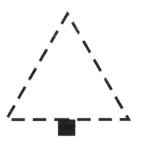

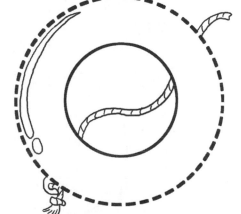

© Marshall Cavendish International (Singapore) Private Limited.

Look at the pictures.
Circle the correct things.

2. the thing that has the shape of a square

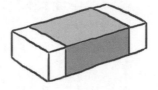

3. the thing that does <u>not</u> have the shape of a circle

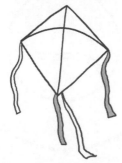

© Marshall Cavendish International (Singapore) Private Limited.

Match.

4.

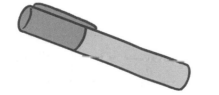

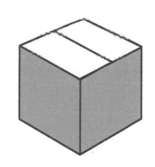

rectangular prism

sphere

cube

cylinder

pyramid

© Marshall Cavendish International (Singapore) Private Limited.

Look at the picture.
Color the shapes in the picture.

5.

Shape	Color
cube	blue
sphere	red
cone	yellow

Shape	Color
pyramid	purple
rectangular prism	green
cylinder	orange

What shape is <u>not</u> in the picture? _____

© Marshall Cavendish International (Singapore) Private Limited.

Practice 7   Making Patterns with Plane Shapes

Sort the shapes.
Write the numbers in the correct boxes.

1.

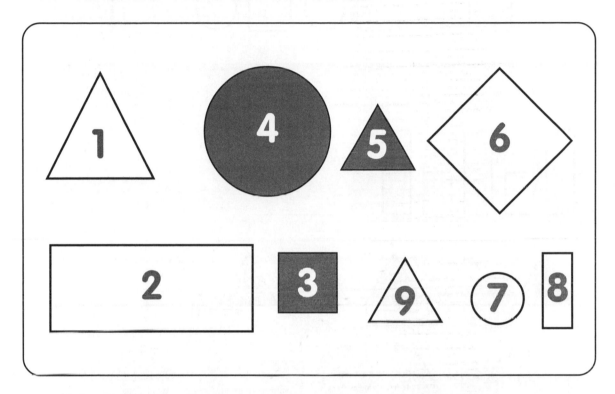

Shape

Circles	Triangles	Squares	Rectangles
4 7			

Size

Big	Small

Color

Black	White

© Marshall Cavendish International (Singapore) Private Limited.

Complete the patterns.
Draw the missing shape.

© Marshall Cavendish International (Singapore) Private Limited.

Example

2.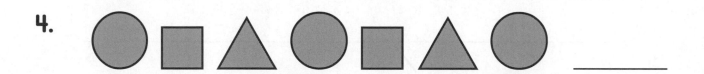

3.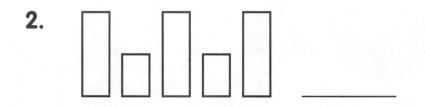

4.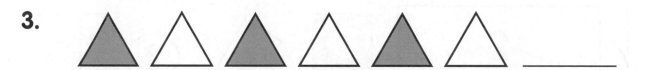

5.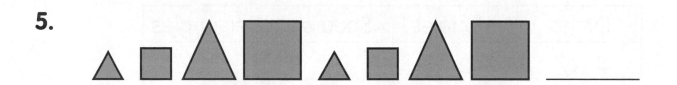

6.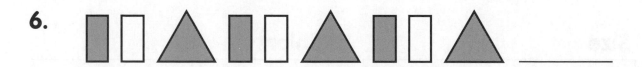

7.

Name: _____   Date: _____

Complete the patterns.
Circle the missing shape.

┌─ **Example** ──┐
│   │
│    ___    │
│   │
└──┘

8.

9.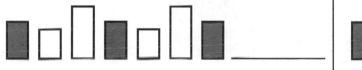

10.

11.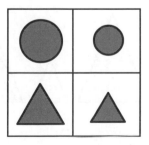

© Marshall Cavendish International (Singapore) Private Limited.

Complete the patterns.
Draw what comes next.

12.

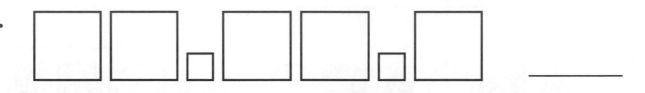

13.

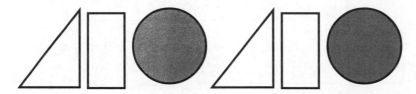

14.

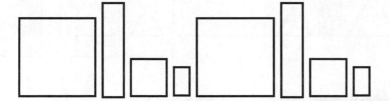

15.

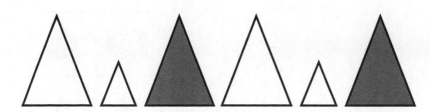

16.

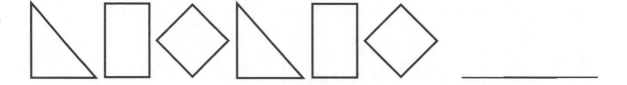

© Marshall Cavendish International (Singapore) Private Limited.

Name: _____   Date: _____

Cut out the shapes below.
Make two patterns.
You do not need to use all the shapes.

17. Paste your first pattern here.

© Marshall Cavendish International (Singapore) Private Limited.

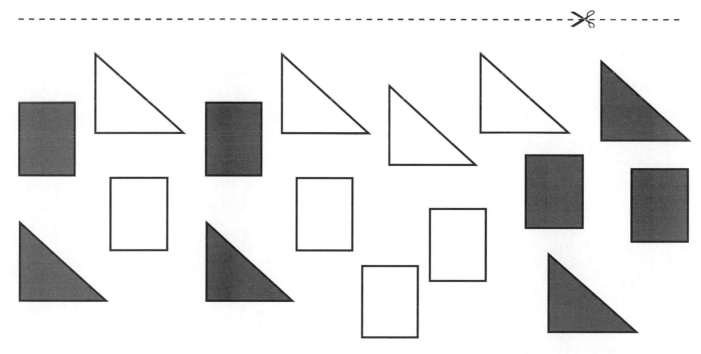

18. Paste your second pattern here.

- ✂ - - - - - - - - - -

© Marshall Cavendish International (Singapore) Private Limited.

Practice 8 Making Patterns with Solid Shapes

Complete the patterns.
Circle the shape that comes next.

1.

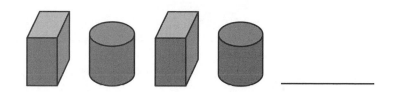 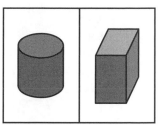

2.

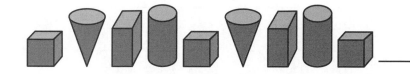

3.

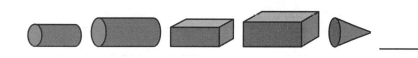 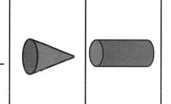

4.

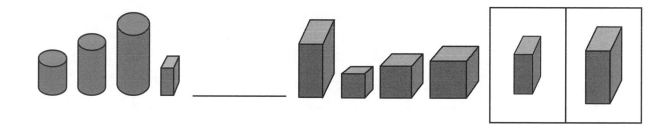

5.

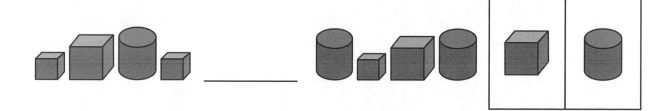

© Marshall Cavendish International (Singapore) Private Limited.

Circle the mistake in the pattern.
Then make a ✔ for the correct shape.

Example

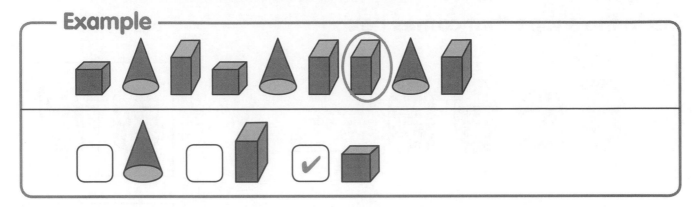

6.

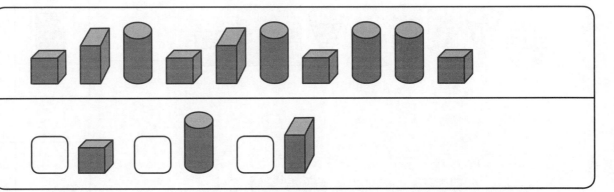

7.

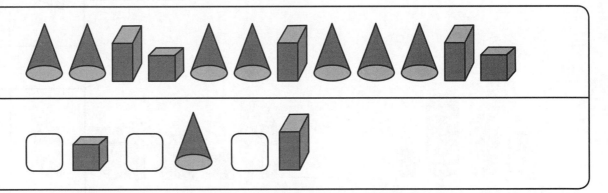

8.

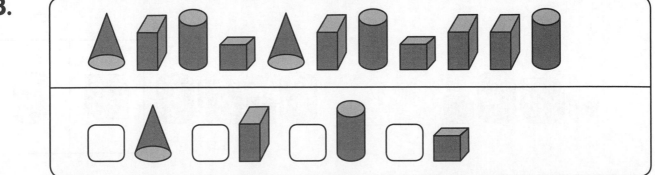

© Marshall Cavendish International (Singapore) Private Limited.

Math Journal

Choose two things.
Circle them.

1.
jar

sharpener
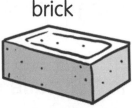

brick
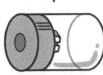

ice-cream
cone

Now write about them.
Use the words in the box to help you.

> cylinder   sphere   cube   cone   pyramid   rectangular prism
>
> stacking   sliding   rolling   size   shape

2.   The _____ has the shape of a _____.

3.   The _____ has the shape of a _____.

4.   I can move the _____ by _____.

5.   I can move the _____ by _____.

Continued on next page

© Marshall Cavendish International (Singapore) Private Limited.

6. My things are alike because they _____

_____.

7. My things are different because they _____

_____.

Make a pattern with plane shapes.
Read and draw.

8. The shapes in this pattern are alike.
The sizes of the shapes are different.

© Marshall Cavendish International (Singapore) Private Limited.

© Marshall Cavendish International (Singapore) Private Limited.

Name: _____   Date: _____

Put On Your Thinking Cap!

Challenging Practice

Solve.

1. Lee, Jen, Bob, and Dean have some shapes.
Find out who has each set of shapes.

- Lee has fewer circles than Bob.

- All of Jen's shapes have 3 sides or more.

- Bob has four kinds of shapes.

- Dean has no squares.

Write the name that matches each set on the line below.

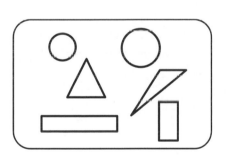

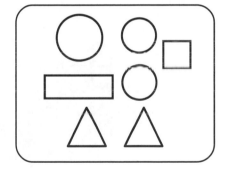

_____

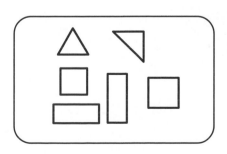

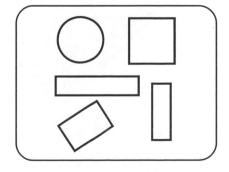

_____

Cut out the pieces of shapes on page 129.
Paste the cut-out pieces to fit the two pictures below.

2.

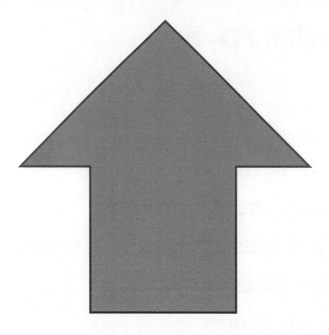

3.

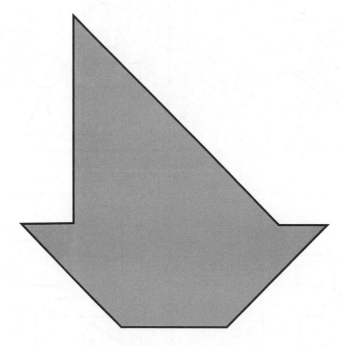

© Marshall Cavendish International (Singapore) Private Limited.

2.

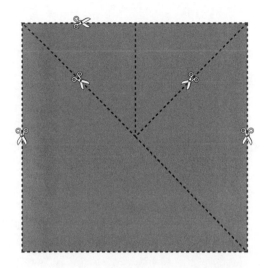

© Marshal Cavendish International (Singapore) Private Limited.

3.

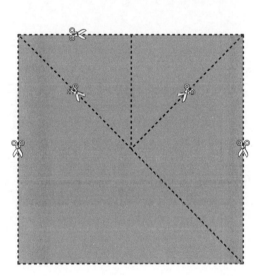

BLANK

Name: _____   Date: _____

Put On Your Thinking Cap!

Problem Solving

Draw and complete the pattern.

Each row (↔) and column (↕) must have these four

shapes, ○ △ □ ▭ .

1.

△	○	▯	☐

© Marshall Cavendish International (Singapore) Private Limited.

Draw and complete the pattern.
Each row (↔) and column must have these four shapes,

2.

			△
○	□	□	
		△	

© Marshall Cavendish International (Singapore) Private Limited.

Chapter Review/Test

Vocabulary

Draw the shape.

1. square

2. rectangle

3. triangle

Write the name.
Use the words in the box.

4.

_____

5.

_____

cylinder
sphere

Concepts and Skills

Trace the shape.
Write the number of sides and corners.

6.

_____ sides

_____ corners

7.

_____ sides

_____ corners

© Marshal Cavendish International (Singapore) Private Limited.

Answer the question.
Write *yes* or *no*.

8.   How are these shapes alike?

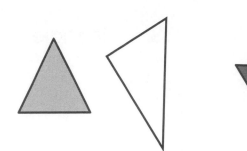 

   a.   same shape _____   **b.** same size _____

   c.   same color _____

Circle the solid shapes you can roll.

9.

How can you move a pyramid?
Circle the answer.

10.

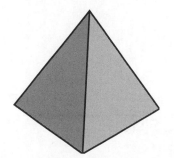

stack

slide

roll

© Marshall Cavendish International (Singapore) Private Limited.

Look at the picture.
What shapes do you see?
Write the number.

11.

square   ⬜

rectangle   ⬜

circle   ⬜

triangle   ⬜

Look at the picture.
What shapes do you see?
Circle the answers.

12.

Plane Shapes	Solid Shapes
circle	sphere
triangle	pyramid
square	cylinder
rectangle	cone
	rectangular prism

© Marshall Cavendish International (Singapore) Private Limited.

Complete the pattern.
Circle the shape that comes next.

13.

14.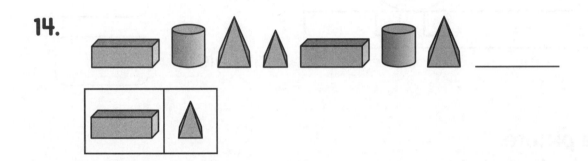

Problem Solving

Draw a line to solve.
Make two shapes that are different in shape and size.

15.

© Marshall Cavendish International (Singapore) Private Limited.

CHAPTER 6 Ordinal Numbers and Position

Practice 1   Ordinal Numbers

Circle.

Example

the 2nd corn

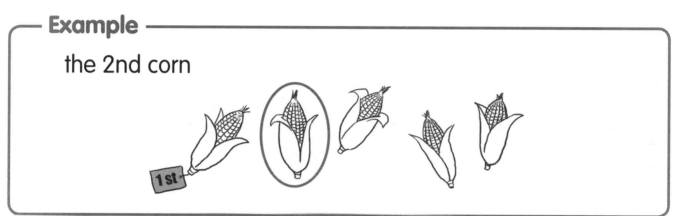

1.   the 5th princess

2.   the 8th bird

3.   the 7th duckling

© Marshall Cavendish International (Singapore) Private Limited.

Color.

4. 3 frogs

the 3rd frog

5. 10 ants

the 10th ant

© Marshall Cavendish International (Singapore) Private Limited.

© Marshall Cavendish International (Singapore) Private Limited.

Name: _____ Date: _____

Match.

6.

 first ● ●  3rd

 second ● ●  5th

 third ● ●  1st

  fourth ● ●  2nd

 fifth ● ●  4th

 sixth ● ●  7th

 seventh ● ●  10th

 eighth ● ●  6th

 ninth ● ●  8th

 tenth ● ● 9th

Look at the picture.
Answer the questions.

7. Who is first in the race? _____

8. Who is fourth in the race? _____

9. In which position is Tandi? _____

10. In which position is Jenn? _____

11. Who is last? _____

© Marshall Cavendish International (Singapore) Private Limited.

Practice 2   Position Words

Look at the picture.
Circle the correct name.

┌─ **Example** ───┐
│   │
│   Who is after Alice?   Carlo   (Ben)   │
│   │
└───┘

1.   Who is before Ben?   Carlo   Alice

2.   Who is after Carlo?   Ben   Denelle

3.   Who is between Eddie and Carlo?   Alice   Denelle

4.   Who is between Carlo and Alice?   Ben   Eddie

© Marshall Cavendish International (Singapore) Private Limited.

Color.

© Marshall Cavendish International (Singapore) Private Limited.

Example

the fourth bird from the left

5. the second pizza from the left

6. the fifth monkey from the right

7. the ninth football from the right

Look at the picture.
Fill in the blanks with the words in the box.

long haired   skinny   fat   big   small

LEFT   RIGHT

| left | right | next to | last |

8.   The long haired dog is first on the _____.

9.   The small dog is _____ from the left.

10. The skinny dog is _____ the fat dog.

11. The big dog is also _____ the fat dog.

Draw.

12. an apple on the last plate from the right
     a banana on the plate next to the apple
     an orange on the sixth plate from the left

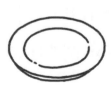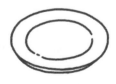

© Marshall Cavendish International (Singapore) Private Limited.

Read the clues to answer the question.
Then write the letters in the correct ☐ **.**

13. What is the capital of the United States of America?

☐ ☐ ☐ ☐ ☐ ☐ ☐ ☐ ☐ ☐ D.C.
a   b   c   d   e   f   g   h   i   j

Clues:

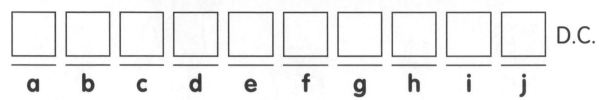

G T H A S N I W O
Left   **Right**

a. second letter from the right

b. fourth letter from the left

c. fifth letter from the left

d. third letter from the left

e. seventh letter from the left

f. fourth letter from the right

g. first letter on the left

h. the letter next to "G"

i. last letter from the left

j. letter between "S" and "I"

© Marshall Cavendish International (Singapore) Private Limited.

Practice 3   Position Words

Color.

1.   the rabbit below the black rabbit pink
       the rabbit above the black rabbit gray
       the rabbit under the paper brown
       the hair of the boy behind the shelf yellow
       the hair of the boy in front of the shelf red

© Marshall Cavendish International (Singapore) Private Limited.

Look at the picture.
Fill in the blanks with the words in the box.

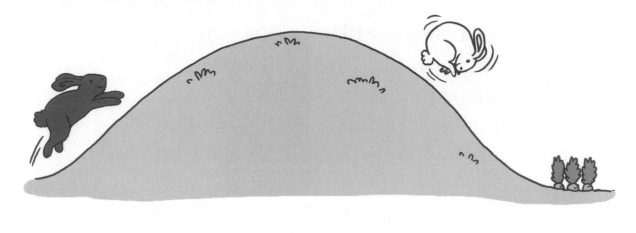

up	near	down	far

2. The black rabbit is hopping _____ the hill.

    The black rabbit is _____ from the carrots.

3. The white rabbit is rolling _____ the hill.

    The white rabbit is _____ the carrots.

© Marshall Cavendish International (Singapore) Private Limited.

Put On Your Thinking Cap!

Challenging Practice

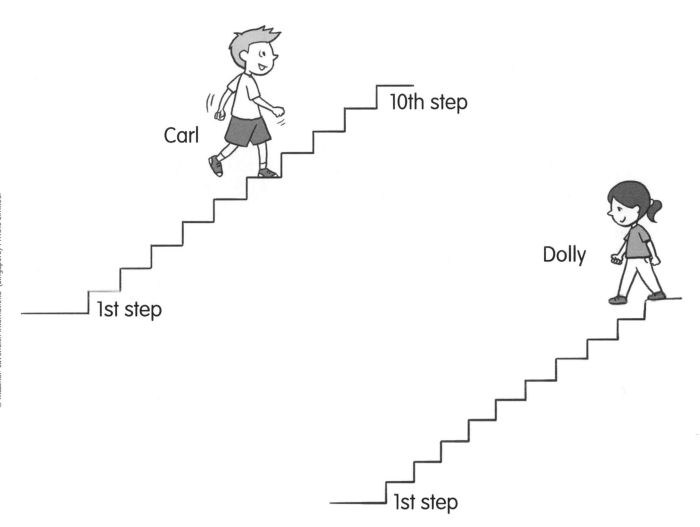

Carl

10th step

1st step

Dolly

1st step

1.   When Carl climbs up four steps, he will be on the tenth step.

Carl is on the _____ step now.

2.   When Dolly walks down three steps, she will be on the
seventh step.

Dolly is on the _____ step now.

© Marshall Cavendish International (Singapore) Private Limited.

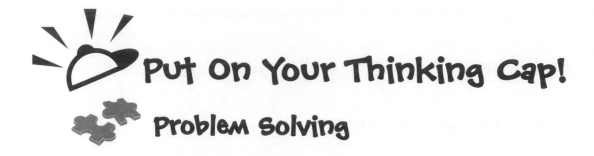
1. There are four rabbits, A, B, C, and D.
   Read the clues.
   Fill in the circles with the correct letters.

Rabbit A is 4th from the right.

Rabbit C is next to Rabbit A.

Rabbit D is between Rabbit C and Rabbit B.

© Marshall Cavendish International (Singapore) Private Limited.

2. Look at the pictures.
Put them in order.
Write the ordinal number that belongs with each picture.

7th	4th	6th	2nd	1st
8th	3rd	9th	5th	10th

© Marshall Cavendish International (Singapore) Private Limited.

3. Michael has some cards in these shapes.

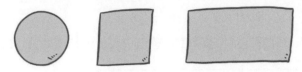

He makes this pattern:

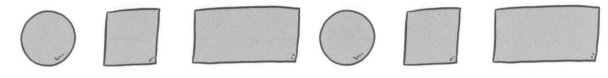

Continue the pattern.
What is the shape of the tenth card from the left?

Draw to find out.

The tenth card from the left is

© Marshall Cavendish International (Singapore) Private Limited.

Chapter Review/Test

Vocabulary

Match.

1. 7th   ●

    3rd   ●

    5th   ●

    10th   ●

    9th   ●

            ●   ninth

            ●   fifth

            ●   seventh

            ●   third

            ●   tenth

Look at the chipmunks.
Where is the acorn?
Circle the correct word.

2.

left   right

3.

under   between

4.

next to   behind

5.

in front of   next to

© Marshall Cavendish International (Singapore) Private Limited.

Concepts and Skills

Read and draw.

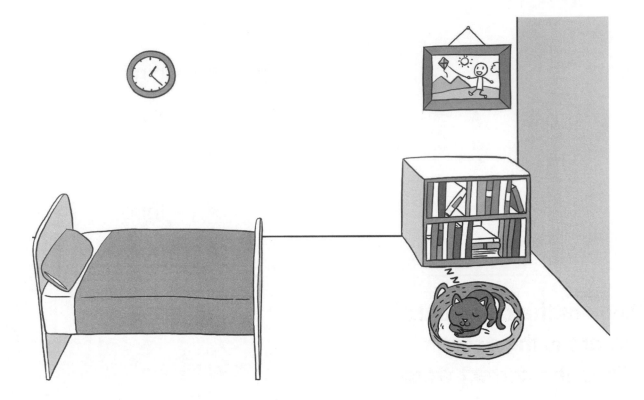

6. The 🧦🧦 are under the bed.

7. The 🐟🥣 is below the picture.

8. The 🐭 is far from the cat.

9. The ⊞ is between the clock and the picture.

10. The 🕷 is above the bed.

11. The ◯ is in front of the cat.

© Marshall Cavendish International (Singapore) Private Limited.

© Marshall Cavendish International (Singapore) Private Limited.

Name: _____   **Date:** _____

Look at the picture.
Fill in the blanks.

| up | after | before | down | between |

12. Ryan is climbing _____ the steps.

13. Gina, Ella, and Brad are sliding _____ the slide.

14. Gina is _____ Ella.

15. Brad is _____ Ella.

16. Ella is _____ Brad and Gina.

Problem Solving

Color.

17.

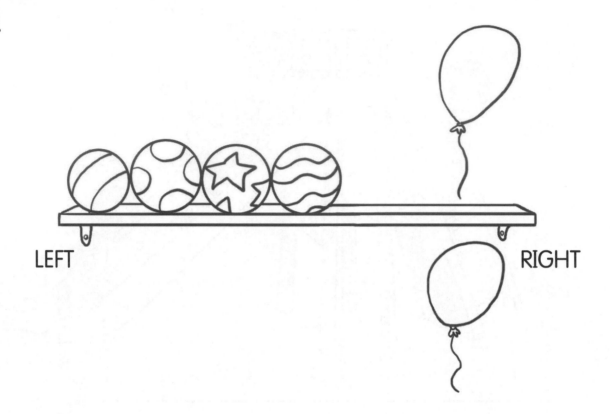

The first ball on the right is blue.

The last ball from the right is orange.

The ball next to the blue ball is red.

The ball between the orange and red ball is green.

The balloon above the shelf is yellow.

The balloon below the shelf is black.

© Marshall Cavendish International (Singapore) Private Limited.

Cumulative Review

for Chapters 5 and 6

Concepts and Skills

Look at the picture.
Count and write the number of shapes you see.

1.

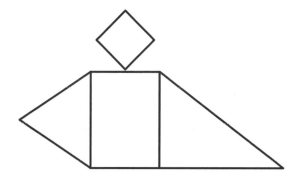

circle ⬚

rectangle ⬚

triangle ⬚

square ⬚

2.

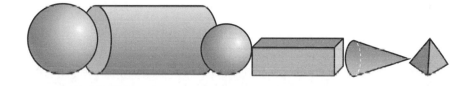

sphere   cylinder   cube

pyramid   rectangular   cone
prism

Find how many sides and corners.

3.

   _____ sides

_____ corners

© Marshall Cavendish International (Singapore) Private Limited.

Sort the shapes by <u>size.</u>
Color the shapes that are <u>different.</u>

4.

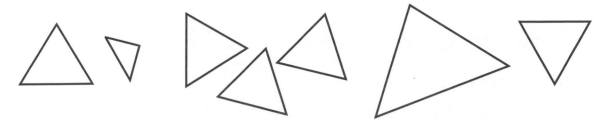

Sort the shapes by the <u>number of sides.</u>
Color the shapes that are <u>alike.</u>

5.

Circle the shapes that roll.

6.

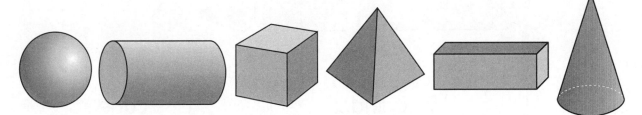

Circle the shapes that stack <u>and</u> slide.

7.

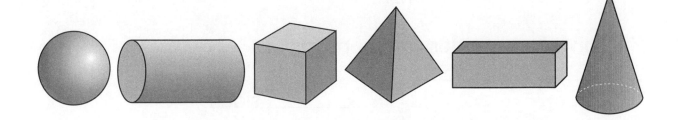

© Marshall Cavendish International (Singapore) Private Limited.

© Marshall Cavendish International (Singapore) Private Limited.

Name: _____   Date: _____

Look at the picture.
Circle the correct shape.

8. The soup can is the shape of a cone   cylinder .

9. The cereal box is the shape of a rectangular prism   rectangle .

10. The roll of paper towel is the shape of a sphere   cylinder .

11. The pizza box top is the shape of a cube   square .

Complete the pattern.
Circle the missing shape.

12.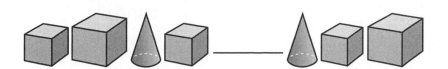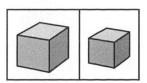

13.

Color.

14. the 3rd sticker

1st

15. the 6th baseball glove

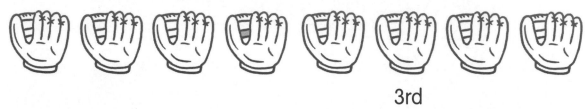

3rd

16. the 10th ladybug

4th

Match.

17.

1st	•	•	third
2nd	•	•	eighth
9th	•	•	second
3rd	•	•	first
8th	•	•	ninth

© Marshall Cavendish International (Singapore) Private Limited.

© Marshall Cavendish International (Singapore) Private Limited.

Name: _____ **Date:** _____

Look at each picture.
Circle the correct word.

18. Andy is (after   before) Eva.

19. Emma is (before   between) Tandi and Mark.

20. Tandi is (after   between) Emma and Mark.

21. Mark is 2nd from the (left   right).

22. Andy is (first   last) on the left.

23. Mark is (in front of   behind) Tandi.

24. Andy is (near   far from) Eva.

Problem Solving

Solve.

25. Shantel draws a rectangle.
    Then she draws a line to make two new shapes.
    The two new shapes are alike.
    Each new shape is the same shape and size.
    Each new shape has 3 corners and 3 sides.

    Draw a line to make the two shapes.

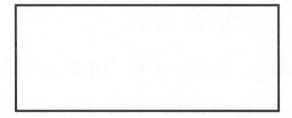

Complete.

26. This is a shape pattern.

    a. Color the 3rd shape.

    b. Draw the next three shapes in the pattern.

    c. Draw the 9th shape.

    d. The 1st shape is a square.
    The 4th shape is a square.

    The _____ shape is also a square.

© Marshall Cavendish International (Singapore) Private Limited.

CHAPTER 7 Numbers to 20

Practice 1   Counting to 20

Write the numbers.

Example

10

11

1.

10

2.

10

© Marshall Cavendish International (Singapore) Private Limited.

3.  10

4.  10

Circle the ten.
Color the rest.
Write the numbers.

© Marshall Cavendish International (Singapore) Private Limited.

Example

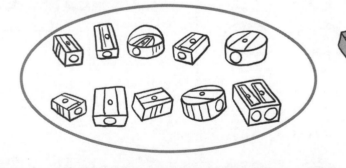

_12_

5.

6.

_____

7.

_____

Fill in the blanks.

8.

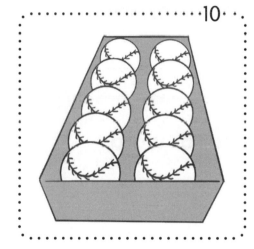

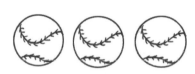

10 and 3 make _____.

10 + 3 = _____

9.

10 and 6 make _____.

10 + 6 = _____

© Marshall Cavendish International (Singapore) Private Limited.

10.

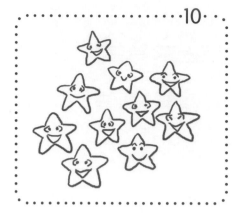

10 and 9 make _____.

10 + 9 = _____

11.

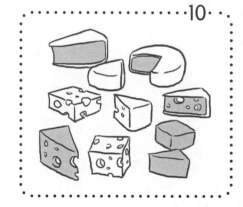

10 and 8 make _____.

10 + 8 = _____

Fill in the blanks with the correct number or word.

12. _____ and _____ make 12.

13. _____ and _____ make 15.

14. _____ is ten and four.

15. _____ is seven and ten.

© Marshall Cavendish International (Singapore) Private Limited.

© Marshall Cavendish International (Singapore) Private Limited.

Name: _____ **Date:** _____

Fill in the blanks.

16. 10 + 3 = _____

17. 10 + 4 = _____

18. 10 + 5 = _____

19. 10 + 6 = _____

20. 10 + 9 = _____

21. 10 + 10 = _____

22. 2 + 10 = _____

23. 8 + 10 = _____

Count.
Circle the correct word.

Example

 10

seven

(eleven)

24.

10

twelve

two

25.

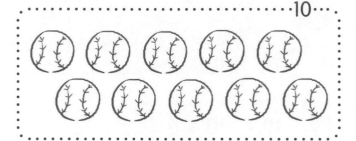

fourteen

fifteen

26.

seventeen

sixteen

27.

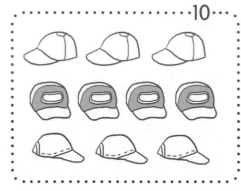

nineteen

twenty

28.

eighteen

twenty

© Marshall Cavendish International (Singapore) Private Limited.

Practice 2   Place Value

Look at the pictures.
Fill in the blanks.

© Marshall Cavendish International (Singapore) Private Limited.

Example

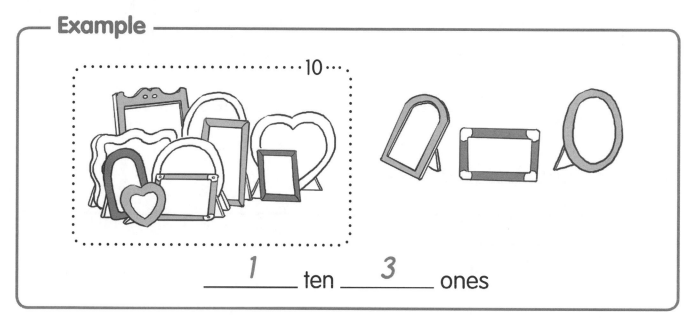

_____ *1* _____ ten   _____ *3* _____ ones

1.

_____ ten _____ ones

2.

_____ ten _____ ones

3.

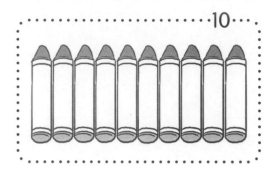

_____ tens _____ ones

Fill in the place-value charts.

Example

	Tens	Ones
19	1	9

4.

	Tens	Ones
11		

5.

	Tens	Ones
12		

6.

	Tens	Ones
15		

7.

	Tens	Ones
20		

© Marshall Cavendish International (Singapore) Private Limited.

Show the number.

Draw | for tens and □ for ones.

Example

Tens	Ones
13	□	□ □ □

8.

Tens	Ones
12		

9.

Tens	Ones
16		

10.

Tens	Ones
18		

11.

Tens	Ones
19		

© Marshall Cavendish International (Singapore) Private Limited.

Look at the place-value charts.
Write the numbers.

12.

Tens	Ones

_____

13.

Tens	Ones

_____

14.

Tens	Ones

_____

15.

Tens	Ones

_____

Fill in the blanks.

16.   13 = 1 ten _____ ones

17.   17 = _____ ten 7 ones

18.   15 = 1 ten _____ ones

19.   12 = _____ ten 2 ones

20.   19 = 1 ten _____ ones

© Marshall Cavendish International (Singapore) Private Limited.

© Marshall Cavendish International (Singapore) Private Limited.

Practice 3   Comparing Numbers

Write the number in each set.
Then fill in the blanks.

Example

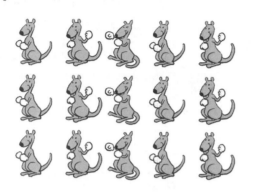 

Set A: _____15_____   Set B: _____12_____

Set _____A_____ has _____3_____ more kangaroos than

Set _____B_____.

1.

Set A: _____   Set B: _____

Set _____ has _____ more penguins than

Set _____.

Write the number in each set.
Then fill in the blanks.

2.

Set A: _____   Set B: _____

Set _____ has _____ more crocodiles than

Set _____.

3.
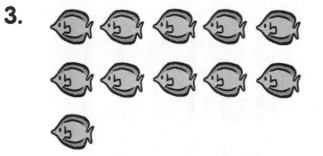 

Set A: _____   Set B: _____

Set _____ has _____ fewer fish than Set _____.

© Marshall Cavendish International (Singapore) Private Limited.

4.

Set A: _____   Set B: _____

Set _____ has _____ fewer butterflies than

Set _____.

5.

Set A: _____   Set B: _____

Set _____ has _____ fewer ants than Set _____.

© Marshall Cavendish International (Singapore) Private Limited.

Color the house with the number that is less.
Then fill in the blanks.

Example

Tens	Ones
▬	◇ ◇ ◇ ◇ ◇
▬	◇ ◇ ◇ ◇ ◇ ◇ ◇ ◇ ◇

_**19**_ is greater than _**16**_.

_**16**_ is less than _**19**_.

The tens are equal.
Compare the ones.
9 ones is greater than
6 ones.
6 ones is less than
9 ones.

6.

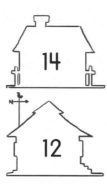

Tens	Ones
▬	◇ ◇ ◇ ◇
▬	◇ ◇

_____ is less than _____.

7.

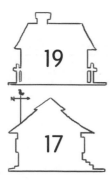

Tens	Ones
▬	◇ ◇ ◇ ◇ ◇ ◇ ◇ ◇ ◇
▬	◇ ◇ ◇ ◇ ◇ ◇ ◇

_____ is greater than _____.

© Marshall Cavendish International (Singapore) Private Limited.

Find the number that is less.
Color the animal red.
Find the number that is greater.
Color the animal blue.

8.

9.

Color the creature with the correct number.
Then fill in the blanks.

10.   the number that is greater

How much greater is the number? _____

© Marshall Cavendish International (Singapore) Private Limited.

11. the number that is less

How much less is the number? _____

Fill in the blanks in each place-value chart.
Then color the sign with the greatest number.

12.

Tens	Ones
1	9
___	___

Tens	Ones
___	___

Tens	Ones
___	___

© Marshall Cavendish International (Singapore) Private Limited.

Fill in the blanks in each place-value chart.
Then color the sign with the least number.

13.

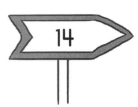

Tens	Ones
_____	_____

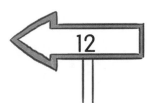

Tens	Ones
_____	_____

Tens	Ones
_____	_____

Compare the numbers.
Fill in the blanks.

14.

_____ is the least number.

_____ is the greatest number.

© Marshall Cavendish International (Singapore) Private Limited.

Compare the numbers.
Fill in the blanks.

15.

_____ is the least number.

_____ is the greatest number.

16.

_____ is the least number.

_____ is the greatest number.

17.

_____ is the least number.

_____ is the greatest number.

© Marshall Cavendish International (Singapore) Private Limited.

Practice 4   Making Patterns and Ordering Numbers

Solve.

1. Alex uses circles to make a pattern.
    How many circles come next in the pattern?
    Draw the circles in the empty box.
    Write the number of circles below this box.

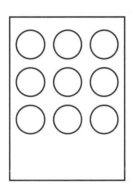 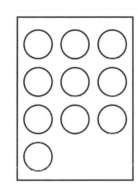 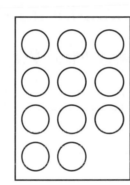 

_____

Complete the patterns.

2.

15   16   17

3.

14   13   12

© Marshall Cavendish International (Singapore) Private Limited.

Look at the numbers.
Fill in the blanks.

4. _____ is 2 more than 15.

5. _____ is 2 less than 20.

6. 1 more than 18 is _____.

7. 2 less than 19 is _____.

Complete the number patterns.

8. | 9 | 11 | | 15 | | 19 |

9. | 12 | | 16 | 18 | |

10. | 19 | 17 | | 13 | | |

11. | 8 | 11 | 14 | | 20 |

12. | 14 | 12 | | 8 | | 4 | |

© Marshall Cavendish International (Singapore) Private Limited.

Help Rosa order the bowling pins and balls.

13. Write the numbers on the  in order from least to greatest.

least

14. Write the numbers on the ⬤ in order from greatest to least.

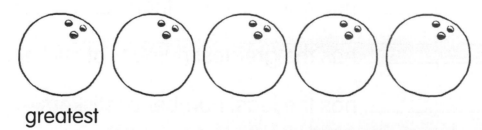

greatest

© Marshall Cavendish International (Singapore) Private Limited.

Math Journal

Count how many stickers the boys have.
Fill in the blanks.

1.

Pete has _____ stickers.   Ty has _____ stickers.

Draw how many stickers you have.
Then fill in the blanks.

2.

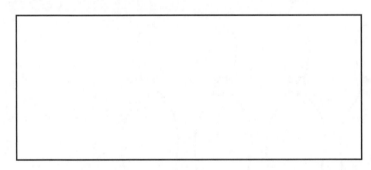

I have _____ stickers.

Write about the number of stickers everyone has.
Fill in the blanks with the correct names.

3. _____ has more stickers than _____.

4. _____ has fewer stickers than _____.

5. _____ has the greatest number of stickers.

6. _____ has the least number of stickers.

© Marshall Cavendish International (Singapore) Private Limited.

Put On Your Thinking Cap!

Challenging Practice

1. Class 1A of Greenfield School holds a basketball contest.
   Find out who won.

   CLUES

   Rita scores the least number of baskets.

   John scores 3 more baskets than Rita.

   Dion scores more baskets than Rachel but less than Frank.

   Write the names next to the number of baskets scored.

   ### Baskets Scored

   _____ 🏀🏀🏀🏀🏀🏀

   _____ 🏀🏀🏀🏀🏀🏀🏀

   _____ 🏀🏀🏀🏀🏀🏀🏀🏀🏀🏀🏀

   _____ 🏀🏀

   _____ 🏀🏀🏀🏀🏀

Who won the contest? _____

© Marshall Cavendish International (Singapore) Private Limited.

Fill in the blanks.

2. 10 + _____ = 15

3. 10 + _____ = 11

4. 10 + _____ = 18

5. _____ + 10 = 14

6. _____ + 10 = 17

Write the correct names.

7. These are the numbers of 12 players on a team.

Roy 19 Bess 5 Shanon 14 Anita 1 Brad 8 Ally 3 Sally 11

Rafer 16 Anuya 0 Robin 20 Ben 7 Seth 10

Whose names have the following numbers?

Numbers less than 5	Numbers from 5 to 9	Numbers from 10 to 14	Numbers from 15 to 20

© Marshall Cavendish International (Singapore) Private Limited.

© Marshall Cavendish International (Singapore) Private Limited.

Name: _____   Date: _____

Put On Your Thinking Cap!

Problem Solving

Use the clues on the next page.
Help Tony find which numbers his counters covered.

Continued on next page

Read what Tony's friends said.

Circle the numbers that were covered on Tony's card.

First, cover the greatest number.

Next, cover the number that is 2 less than the greatest number.

Then, cover the number that is the least.

There are two more numbers. I remember that one of these numbers is 3 less than the other.

Tony's card.

1	9	13	18
5	3	7	17
16	11	15	12

© Marshall Cavendish International (Singapore) Private Limited.

© Marshell Cavendish International (Singapore) Private Limited.

Name: _____   Date: _____

Chapter Review/Test

Vocabulary

Unscramble the letters to spell each number.

1.   15   f i e e t f n

_____

2.   11   e v l e e n

_____

3.   18   e g e e t h n i

_____

4.   20   t w y n e t

_____

Fill in the blank with the correct word.

place-value chart   compare

5.   You can show numbers as tens and ones in

a _____.

6.   When you _____ 12 and 15, 12 is the number that is less.

Concepts and Skills

Count. Write the number.

7.

_____ puppets

8.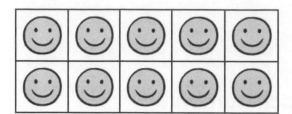

_____ faces.

Fill in the blanks.

9.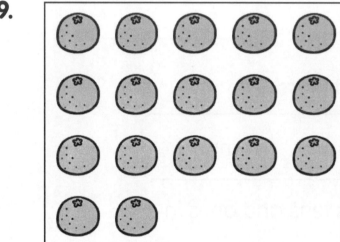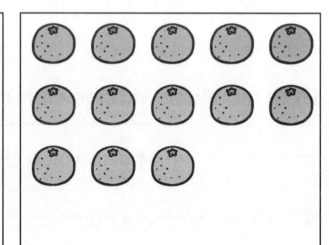

Set A: _____   Set B: _____

Set _____ has _____ more oranges than Set _____.

Set _____ has _____ fewer oranges than Set _____.

Which is the greater number? _____

Complete the number pattern.

10. 13, 14, _____, _____, 17, _____, 19

11. 19, 17, _____, 13, 11, _____

© Marshall Cavendish International (Singapore) Private Limited.

© Marshall Cavendish International (Singapore) Private Limited.

Name: _____ **Date:** _____

Write the numbers in order from least to greatest.

12.

| 17 | 3 | 0 | 10 | 15 |

_____ , _____ , _____ , _____ , _____

Write the numbers in order from greatest to least.

13.

| 11 | 19 | 8 | 9 | 14 |

_____ , _____ , _____ , _____ , _____

Problem Solving

Read the clues.
Then cross out the numbers to solve.

__ Example __

| 1̶0̶ | 1̶1̶ | 1̶2̶ | 1̶3̶ | 1̶4̶ | 15 | 1̶6̶ | 1̶7̶ | 1̶8̶ | 1̶9̶ | 2̶0̶ |

I am greater than 13.
I am less than 17.
Of the numbers that are left:
    I am not the least.
    I am not the greatest.
What number am I? _____ *15*

14.

10	11	12	13	14	15	16	17	18	19	20

I am less than 20.

I am more than 13.

I am less than 17.

I am 4 more than 12.

What number am I? _____

15.

10	11	12	13	14	15	16	17	18	19	20

a. I am more than 10.

I am less than 20.

I am more than 12.

I am less than 15.

Of the numbers that are left:

I am the greater number.

What number am I? _____

b. Draw the number in the place-value chart.

Draw ▯ for tens and □ for ones.

Tens	Ones

© Marshall Cavendish International (Singapore) Private Limited.

© Marshall Cavendish International (Singapore) Private Limited.

Name: _____ **Date:** _____

Addition and Subtraction Facts to 20

Practice 1   Ways to Add

Make a 10.
Then add.

Example

$8 + 6 =$ _____10_____ + _____4_____

$=$ _____14_____

1.

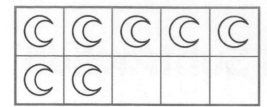

$7 + 5 = \underline{\hspace{2cm}} + \underline{\hspace{2cm}}$

$ = \underline{\hspace{2cm}}$

2.

$9 + 6 = \underline{\hspace{2cm}} + \underline{\hspace{2cm}}$

$ = \underline{\hspace{2cm}}$

© Marshall Cavendish International (Singapore) Private Limited.

© Marshall Cavendish International (Singapore) Private Limited.

Name: _____ **Date:** _____

Draw 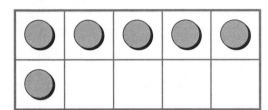 in the ☐☐☐☐☐ to make a 10.

Then add.

Example

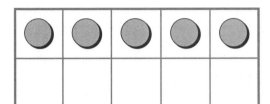

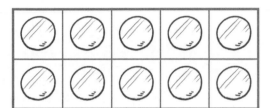

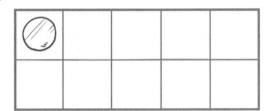

$6 + 5 = \underline{\quad 10 \quad} + \underline{\quad 1 \quad}$

$= \underline{\quad 11 \quad}$

3.

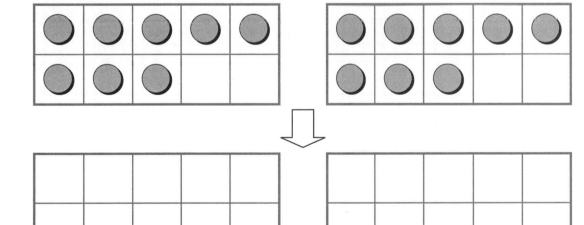

$8 + 8 = \underline{\qquad} + \underline{\qquad}$

$= \underline{\qquad}$

4.

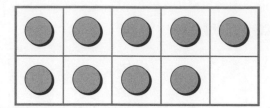 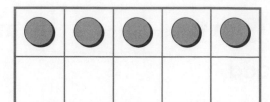

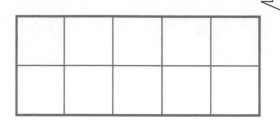

$9 + 5 =$ _____ $+$ _____

$=$ _____

5.

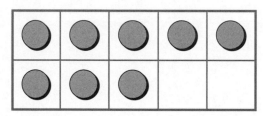 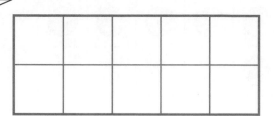

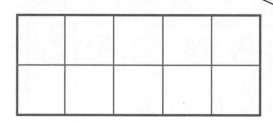

$8 + 7 =$ _____ $+$ _____

$=$ _____

© Marshall Cavendish International (Singapore) Private Limited.

© Marshall Cavendish International (Singapore) Private Limited.

Name: _____   **Date:** _____

Draw ⬤ in the ☐☐☐☐☐ to show the numbers.

Then draw ⬤ in the ☐☐☐☐☐ and add.

Example

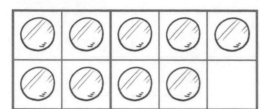 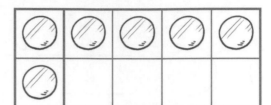

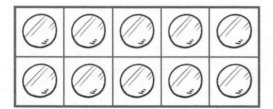 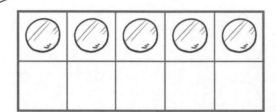

9 + 6 = ___10___ + ___5___

= ___15___

6.

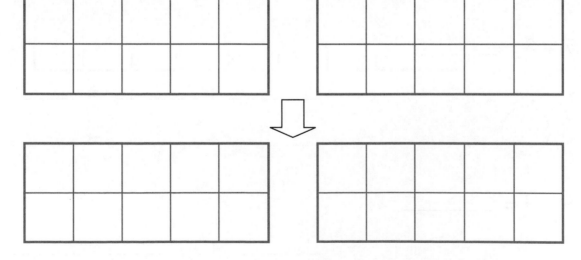

7 + 6 = _____ + _____

= _____

Make a 10.
Then add.

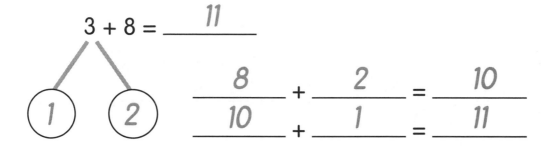

Example

$3 + 8 =$ ___11___

$$\frac{8}{10} + \frac{2}{1} = \frac{10}{11}$$

$$\text{___} 10 \text{___} + \text{___} 1 \text{___} = \text{___} 11 \text{___}$$

7. $5 + 9 =$ _____

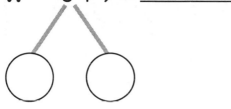

_____ + _____ = _____

_____ + _____ = _____

8. $6 + 6 =$ _____

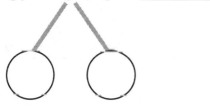

_____ + _____ = _____

_____ + _____ = _____

9. $7 + 8 =$ _____

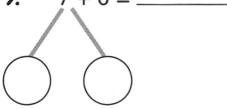

_____ + _____ = _____

_____ + _____ = _____

10. $9 + 9 =$ _____

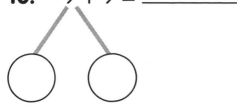

_____ + _____ = _____

_____ + _____ = _____

Name: _____ Date: _____

Practice 2   Ways to Add

Group the numbers into a 10 and ones.
Then add.

┌─ **Example** ──────────────────────────────────────┐

$$12 + 5 = \underline{\quad 17 \quad}$$

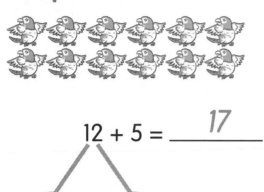

⑩   ②

└──┘

1.

$$12 + 3 = \underline{\qquad\qquad}$$

○   ○

2.

$$11 + 5 = \underline{\qquad\qquad}$$

○   ○

© Marshall Cavendish International (Singapore) Private Limited.

3.

$$14 + 3 = \underline{\hspace{2cm}}$$

4.

$$8 + 11 = \underline{\hspace{2cm}}$$

Add.

5. $15 + 2 = \underline{\hspace{2cm}}$

6. $12 + 4 = \underline{\hspace{2cm}}$

7. $13 + 5 = \underline{\hspace{2cm}}$

8. $6 + 11 = \underline{\hspace{2cm}}$

9. $7 + 12 = \underline{\hspace{2cm}}$

10. $7 + 11 = \underline{\hspace{2cm}}$

© Marshall Cavendish International (Singapore) Private Limited.

Name: _____ Date: _____

Practice 3 Ways to Add

Complete each addition sentence.

© Marshall Cavendish International (Singapore) Private Limited.

> **Example**
>
> What is double 1?
>
>
>
> Double 1 means to add _____*1*_____ more to 1.
>
> 1 + _____*1*_____ = _____*2*_____

1. What is double 2?

Double 2 means to add _____ more to 2.

_____ + _____ = _____

2. What is double 3?

Double 3 means to add _____ more to 3.

_____ + _____ = _____

3. 4 + 4 = _____

4. 5 + 5 = _____

Complete each addition sentence.

5.   **a.**   3 + 3 = _____

              3 + 4 = _____

     b.   3 + 3 is double _____.

              3 + 4 is double _____ plus _____.

Complete the number bonds.
Then fill in the blanks.

© Marshall Cavendish International (Singapore) Private Limited.

— **Example** —

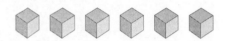

6 + 7 = ?

   6   **1**

6 + 7 is double 6 plus ___*1*___.

6 + 6 + ___*1*___

= 12 + ___*1*___

= 13

6.   7 + 8 = ?

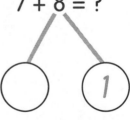

             1

7 + 8 is double _____ plus 1.

7 + _____ + 1

= _____ + 1

= 15

7.   5 + 4 = ?

5 + 4 is double _____ plus 1.

_____ + _____ + _____

= _____

Use doubles facts to complete the addition sentences.

┌─── **Example** ───────────────────────────┐
│ ⌐2⌐ + ⌐2⌐ = 4   │
└──┘

8. ☐ + ☐ = 0

9. ☐ + ☐ = 12

10. ☐ + ☐ = 10

11. ☐ + ☐ = 16

12. ☐ + ☐ = 18

13. ☐ + ☐ = 20

© Marshall Cavendish International (Singapore) Private Limited.

Add the doubles-plus one numbers.
Use doubles facts to help you.
Then write the doubles fact you used.

> **Example**
>
> 5 + 6 = _____11_____
>
> Doubles fact: ____5____ + ____5____ = ____10____

14.   7 + 6 = _____

   Doubles fact: _____ + _____ = _____

15.   7 + 8 = _____

   Doubles fact: _____ + _____ = _____

16.   9 + 10 = _____

   Doubles fact: _____ + _____ = _____

17.   8 + 9 = _____

   Doubles fact: _____ + _____ = _____

© Marshall Cavendish International (Singapore) Private Limited.

Practice 4   Ways to Subtract

Group the numbers into a 10 and ones.
Then subtract.

Example

$$13 - 2 = \underline{\quad 11 \quad}$$

(10)   (3)

1.

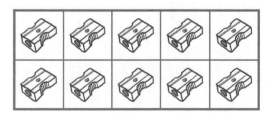

$$17 - 3 = \underline{\qquad}$$

◯   ◯

2.

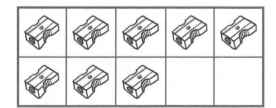

$$18 - 0 = \underline{\qquad}$$

◯   ◯

© Marshall Cavendish International (Singapore) Private Limited.

3.

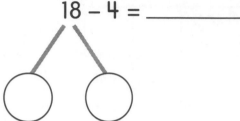

$18 - 4 = $ _____

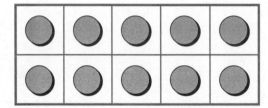

_____ $-$ _____ $=$ _____

_____ $+$ _____ $=$ _____

4.

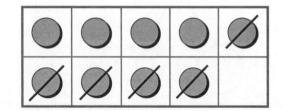

$19 - 5 = $ _____

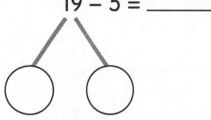

_____ $-$ _____ $=$ _____

_____ $+$ _____ $=$ _____

5.

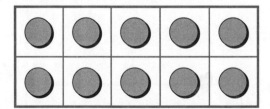

$17 - 6 = $ _____

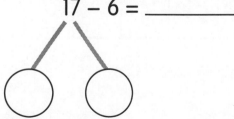

_____ $-$ _____ $=$ _____

_____ $+$ _____ $=$ _____

© Marshall Cavendish International (Singapore) Private Limited.

© Marshall Cavendish International (Singapore) Private Limited.

Name: _____   Date: _____

Group the numbers into a 10 and ones.
Then subtract.

Example

$13 - 1 = \underline{12}$

$\underline{3} - \underline{1} = \underline{2}$

$\underline{10} + \underline{2} = \underline{12}$

6. $14 - 2 = \underline{}$

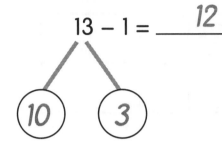

$\underline{} - \underline{} = \underline{}$

$\underline{} + \underline{} = \underline{}$

7. $15 - 3 = \underline{}$

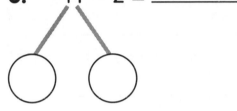

$\underline{} - \underline{} = \underline{}$

$\underline{} + \underline{} = \underline{}$

8. $16 - 3 = \underline{}$

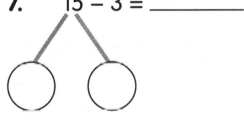

$\underline{} - \underline{} = \underline{}$

$\underline{} + \underline{} = \underline{}$

9. $19 - 3 = \underline{}$

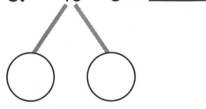

$\underline{} - \underline{} = \underline{}$

$\underline{} + \underline{} = \underline{}$

Group the numbers into a 10 and ones.
Then subtract.

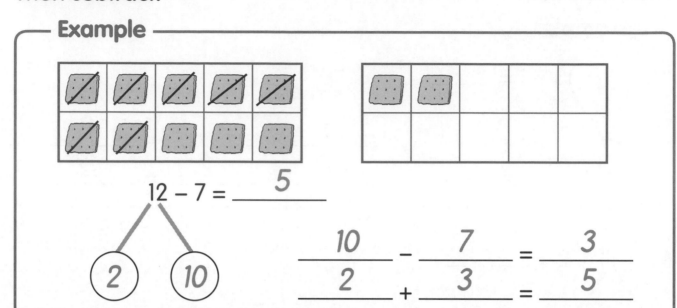

Example

$$12 - 7 = \underline{\quad 5 \quad}$$

2   10

$$\frac{10}{2} - \frac{7}{} = \frac{3}{}$$
$$\underline{} + \underline{3} = \underline{5}$$

10.

$$15 - 6 = \underline{\qquad}$$

$$\underline{\qquad} - \underline{\qquad} = \underline{\qquad}$$
$$\underline{\qquad} + \underline{\qquad} = \underline{\qquad}$$

© Marshall Cavendish International (Singapore) Private Limited.

11.

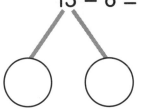   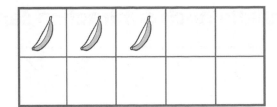

$13 - 8 =$ _____

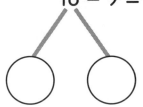

_____ − _____ = _____

_____ + _____ = _____

12.

    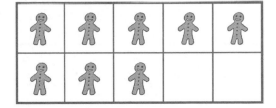

$12 - 6 =$ _____

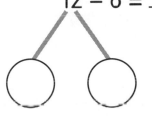

_____ − _____ = _____

_____ + _____ = _____

13.

$18 - 9 =$ _____

_____ − _____ = _____

_____ + _____ = _____

© Marshall Cavendish International (Singapore) Private Limited.

Complete each subtraction sentence.

14.

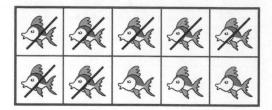

$$16 - 7 = \underline{\hspace{2cm}}$$

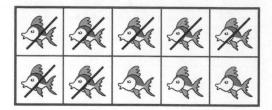

15.

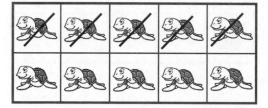

$$14 - \underline{\hspace{2cm}} = \underline{\hspace{2cm}}$$

16.

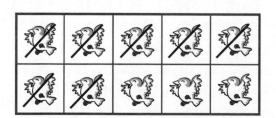

$$\underline{\hspace{2cm}} - 7 = \underline{\hspace{2cm}}$$

© Marshall Cavendish International (Singapore) Private Limited.

© Marshall Cavendish International (Singapore) Private Limited.

Complete each subtraction sentence.

17.

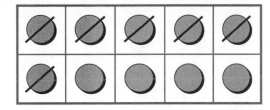

_____ − _____ = _____

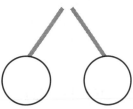

18.

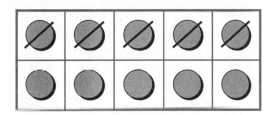

_____ − _____ = _____

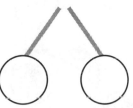

19.

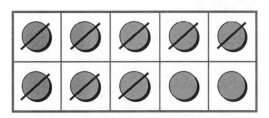

_____ − _____ = _____

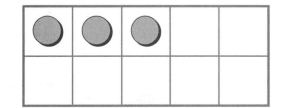

Complete the number bonds.
Subtract.

20. 16 – 6 = _____

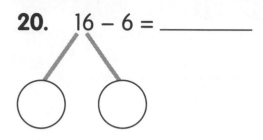

21. 14 – 7 = _____

Solve.

22. Which number fell into the number machine?
Write the number in ◯.

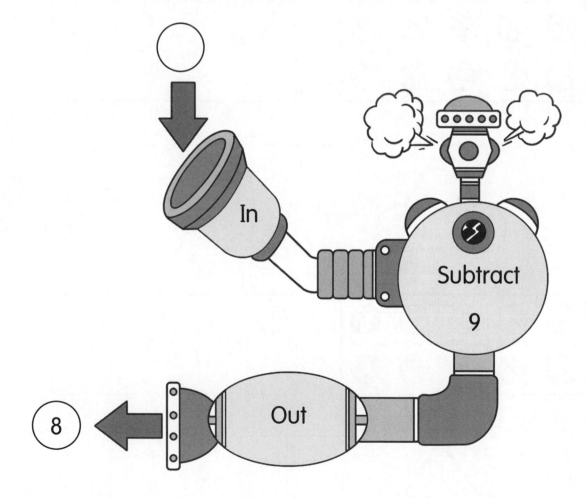

© Marshall Cavendish International (Singapore) Private Limited.

© Marshall Cavendish International (Singapore) Private Limited.

Practice 5   Real-World Problems: Addition and Subtraction Facts

Solve.

1.   Mandy has 5 toy bears.
     She has 5 toy dogs.
     How many toys does she
     have in all?

Mandy has _____ toys in all.

2.   6 children are on the
     merry-go-round.
     6 more children join them.
     How many children are
     there now?

There are _____ children now.

3.   Sam has 8 marbles.
     Lamont gives him 9 marbles.
     How many marbles does Sam
     have now?

Sam has _____ marbles now.

4. Sue has 13 green ribbons
and red ribbons.
5 ribbons are green.
How many red ribbons
does Sue have?

Sue has _____ red ribbons.

5. Malika makes 12 bracelets.
She sells some bracelets.
She has 4 bracelets left.
How many bracelets does
Malika sell?

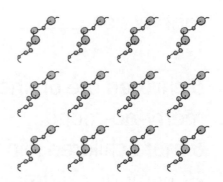

Malika sells _____ bracelets.

6. Al makes 16 butterfly knots.
He gives 9 butterfly knots to
his friends.
How many butterfly knots
does Al have left?

Al has _____ butterfly knots left.

© Marshall Cavendish International (Singapore) Private Limited.

 Put On Your Thinking Cap!

 Challenging Practice

Write + or − in each circle.

1. $10 \bigcirc 6 = 4$

2. $7 \bigcirc 5 = 12$

3. $16 \bigcirc 9 = 7$

4. $9 \bigcirc 7 = 16$

5. $11 \bigcirc 3 = 14$

6. $14 \bigcirc 6 = 20$

7. $17 \bigcirc 2 = 15$

8. $12 \bigcirc 8 = 20$

Fill in the blanks.

9. $18 - \underline{\hspace{2cm}} = 10$

10. $\underline{\hspace{2cm}} - 9 = 11$

11. $20 - \underline{\hspace{2cm}} = 20$

12. $\underline{\hspace{2cm}} - 6 = 6$

13. $\underline{\hspace{2cm}} + 3 = 12$

14. $\underline{\hspace{2cm}} + 5 = 13$

© Marshall Cavendish International (Singapore) Private Limited.

Solve.

15.   Dane gets 2 baskets in a computer game.
His total score is 16.

a.   Color 2 baskets that he gets.

b.   Which are the 2 baskets that he got?
Write an addition sentence for them.

_____ + _____ = 16

c.   Look for other answers.
Write them here.

_____ + _____ = 16

_____ + _____ = 16

© Marshall Cavendish International (Singapore) Private Limited.

© Marshall Cavendish International (Singapore) Private Limited.

Put On Your Thinking Cap!

Problem Solving

Solve.

Ed did 6 more cartwheels than Lila.
How many cartwheels did
Ed and Lila each do?

Write four possible pairs of numbers.
The total number of cartwheels cannot be more than 20.

1.　If Lila did _____ cartwheels, then Ed did _____
　　cartwheels.

2.　If Lila did _____ cartwheels, then Ed did _____
　　cartwheels.

3.　If Ed did _____ cartwheels, then Lila did _____
　　cartwheels.

4.　If Ed did _____ cartwheels, then Lila did _____
　　cartwheels.

Fill the ◯ with any of these numbers.

Use each number once.

5.

| 2 | 3 | 5 | 6 |

The numbers in each line must add up to 12. For example, 1 + 4 + 7 = 12

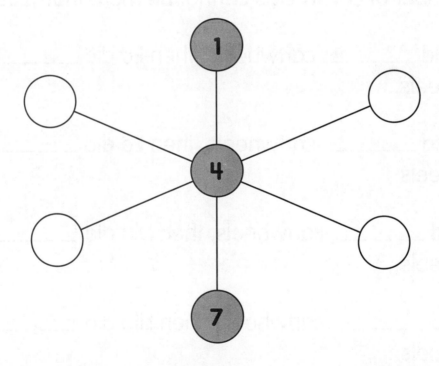

© Marshall Cavendish International (Singapore) Private Limited.

© Marshall Cavendish International (Singapore) Private Limited.

Chapter Review/Test

Vocabulary

Circle the correct answers.

1. Which numbers are the <u>same</u>?

    4   9   6   0   4

2. Which fact is a doubles fact?

    9 + 1 = 10   4 + 8 = 12   9 + 9 = 18

3. Which fact is a doubles plus one fact?

    1 + 2 = 3   3 + 3 = 6   9 + 2 = 11

Concepts and Skills

Fill in the blanks.

4. 6 + 5 = _____   5. 9 + 6 = _____

Complete the number bonds.
Then fill in the blanks.

6. 15 + 4 = _____   7. 6 + 14 = _____

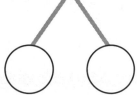

8. 16 − 4 = _____   9. 14 − 8 = _____

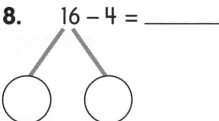

Fill in the blanks.

10. 11 + 9 = _____

11. 12 − 5 = _____

Problem Solving

Solve.

12. Andy has 9 stickers.
His sister gives him 5 more.
How many stickers does
Andy have in all?

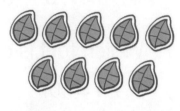

Andy has _____ stickers in all.

13. Tia has 14 hair clips.
She gives 7 hair clips to her sister.
How many hair clips does Tia
have left?

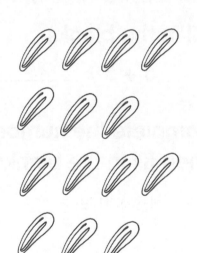

Tia has _____ hair clips left.

14. I am double 6 plus 1 more.
What number am I?

I am the number _____.

© Marshall Cavendish International (Singapore) Private Limited.

CHAPTER 9 Length

Practice 1 Comparing Two Things

Circle the correct answer.

— **Example** —

Which is longer?

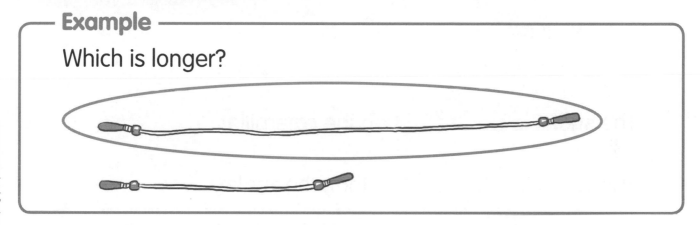

1. Who is taller?

2. Which is shorter?

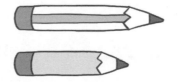

© Marshall Cavendish International (Singapore) Private Limited.

Fill in the blanks.

© Marshall Cavendish International (Singapore) Private Limited.

> **Example**
>
> Which is longer?
> Which is shorter?
>
>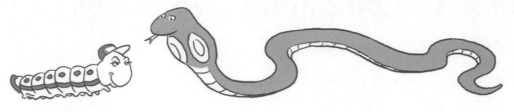
>
> caterpillar   snake
>
> The snake is _longer_ than the caterpillar.
>
> The caterpillar is _shorter_ than the snake.

3. Which is shorter?
    Which is taller?

The giraffe is _____ than the tree.

The tree is _____ than the giraffe.

4. Which is longer?
Which is shorter

The train is _____ than the truck.

The truck is _____ than the train.

5. Which is shorter?
Which is taller?

swan   duck

The duck is _____ than the swan.

The swan is _____ than the duck.

© Marshall Cavendish International (Singapore) Private Limited.

Draw.

Example

a longer arrow

———————————▶

———————————▶

6.   a shorter tree

7.   a longer and taller ship

© Marshall Cavendish International (Singapore) Private Limited.

Name: _____ Date: _____

Practice 2   Comparing More Than Two Things

Look at the picture.
Fill in the blanks with the correct names.

Rolo   Lad   Biff

1.   _____ is taller than Biff.

2.   Biff is taller than _____.

3.   So, Lad is also taller than _____.

Read.
Then draw the tails on the mouse and dog.

4.   The mouse's tail is longer than the cat's tail.
     The cat's tail is longer the dog's tail.
     So, the mouse's tail is longer than the dog's tail.

© Marshall Cavendish International (Singapore) Private Limited.

Color.

─ **Example** ─────────────────────

the longest string of beads

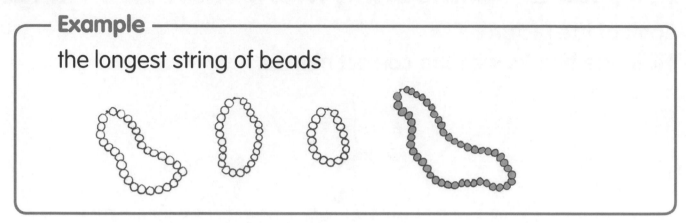

5. the shortest vegetable

6. the girl with the longest hair

7. the tallest animal

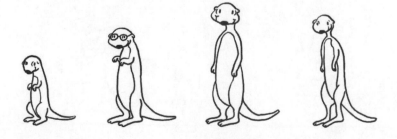

© Marshall Cavendish International (Singapore) Private Limited.

© Marshall Cavendish International (Singapore) Private Limited.

Name: _____   Date: _____

Fill in the blanks with *taller, tallest, shorter,* or *shortest*.

ostrich   elephant   bear   giraffe

8.   The giraffe is the _____ animal.

9.   The ostrich is _____ than the bear.

10.   The _____ animal is the bear.

11.   The ostrich is _____ than the elephant.

Look at the picture.
Fill in the blanks.

   very curly wire

   curly wire

_____   straight wire

12.   The _____ is longer than the curly wire.

13.   The curly wire is longer than the _____.

14.   The _____ is the longest wire.

Math Journal

Help Jamie put his toys away. Read.
Then cut out the toys on page 227 and paste them on the shelf.

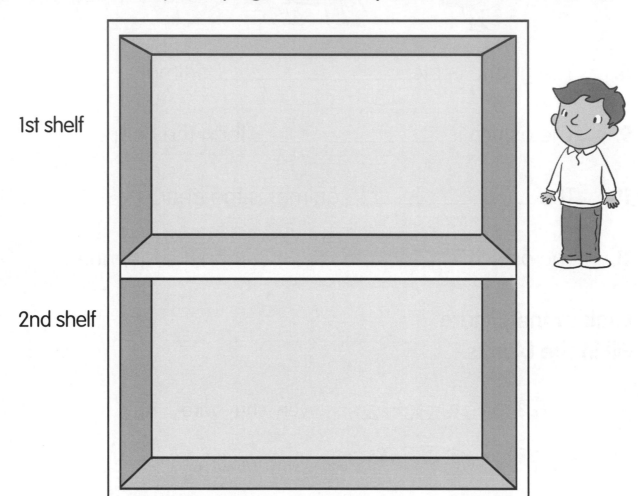

1st shelf	• teddy bear • toy taller than the teddy bear
2nd shelf	• toy shorter than the teddy bear • longest toy • toy shorter than the toy train

© Marshall Cavendish International (Singapore) Private Limited.

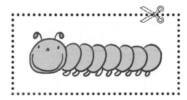

© Marshall Cavendish International (Singapore) Private Limited.

BLANK

Practice 3   Using A Start Line

Cut out the caterpillars.
Paste them on the box in the order shown.

1.

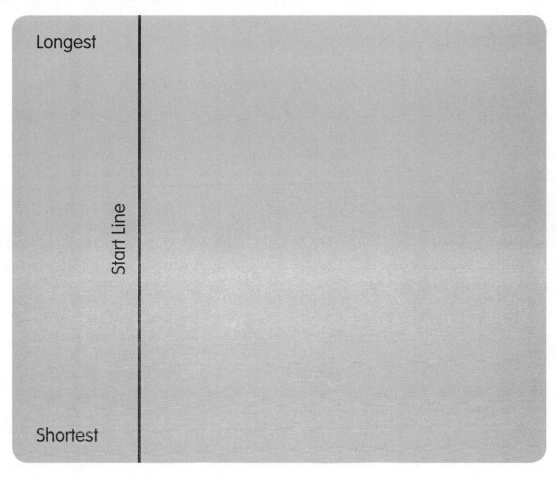

© Marshall Cavendish International (Singapore) Private Limited.

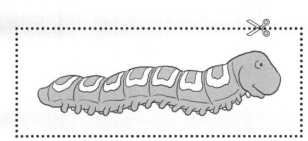

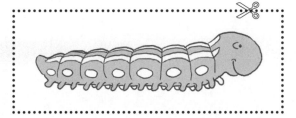

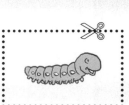

Draw 2 more pencils.
Color the longest pencil blue.
Color the shortest pencil green.

2.   Start Line

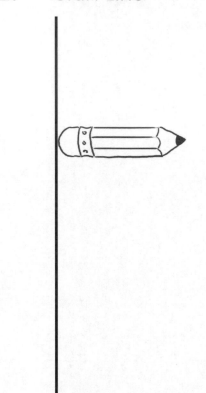

© Marshall Cavendish International (Singapore) Private Limited.

Practice 4   Measuring Things

Count.
Fill in the blanks.

Example

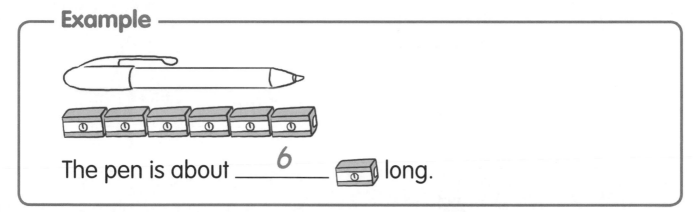

The pen is about _____6_____ long.

1.

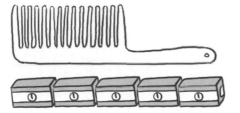

The comb is about _____ 🔲 long.

2.

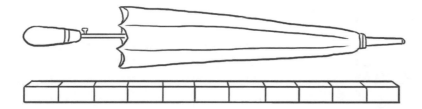

The umbrella is about _____ ▱ long.

© Marshall Cavendish International (Singapore) Private Limited.

3.

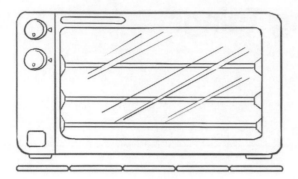

The oven is about _____  long.

4.

The photo frame is about _____ 〰 long.

5.

The envelope is about _____ 〰 long.

© Marshall Cavendish International (Singapore) Private Limited.

Fill in the blanks.

What is the length of each tape?

┌─ **Example** ────────────────────────────────────┐

 tape

 buttons
pegs

The tape is about ____8____ buttons long.

It is about ____2____ pegs long.

└──┘

6.

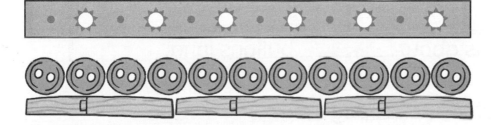

The tape is about _____ buttons long.

It is about _____ pegs long.

7.

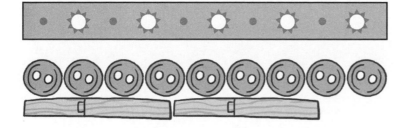

The tape is about _____ buttons long.

It is about _____ pegs long.

© Marshall Cavendish International (Singapore) Private Limited.

8.

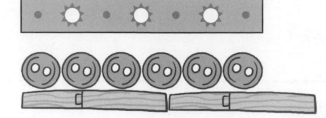

The tape is about _____ buttons long.

It is about _____ pegs long.

9.

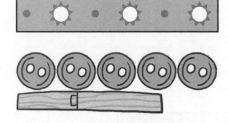

The tape is about _____ buttons long.

It is about _____ peg long.

© Marshall Cavendish International (Singapore) Private Limited.

Practice 5   Finding Length in Units

Count.
Fill in the blanks.

> ### Example
>
> 1 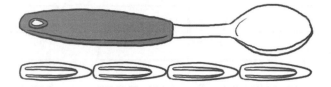 stands for 1 unit.
>
>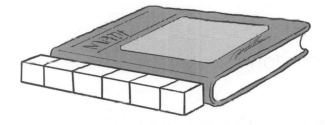
>
> The spoon is about ____4____ units long.

1.   1 ⬜ stands for 1 unit.

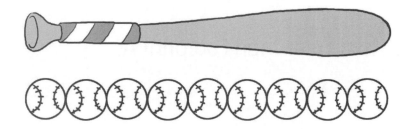

The book is about _____ units long.

2.   1 ⚾ stands for 1 unit.

The bat is about _____ units long.

© Marshall Cavendish International (Singapore) Private Limited.

Look at the picture.
Fill in the blanks.

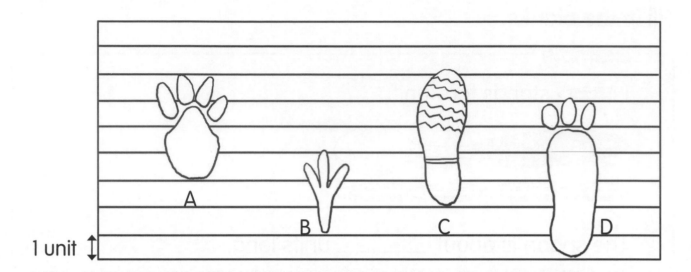

1 unit

3.   Footprint A is _____4_____ units long.

4.   Footprint B is _____ units long.

5.   Footprint C is _____ units long.

6.   Footprint D is _____ units long.

7.   Footprint _____ is the longest.

8.   Footprint _____ is shorter than Footprint A.

© Marshall Cavendish International (Singapore) Private Limited.

Look at the picture.
Fill in the blanks.

1 ▢ stands for 1 unit.

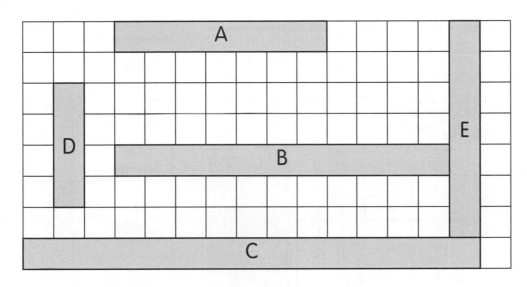

9.   Strip _____ is the longest.

It is _____ units long.

This is _____ ten and _____ ones.

10.   Strip _____ is the shortest.

It is _____ units long.

11.   Strip _____ is as long as Strip _____.

12.   Strip _____ is shorter than Strip C but longer than Strip E.

It is _____ units long.

This is _____ ten and _____ one.

© Marshall Cavendish International (Singapore) Private Limited.

Look at the picture.
Fill in the blanks. Use numbers or the words in the box.

1 ⬜ stands for 1 unit.

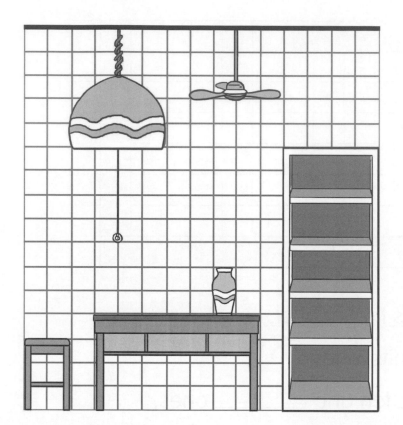

short

shorter

shortest

taller

tallest

longer

longest

13. The table is _____ units long.

14. The bookshelf is _____ units tall.

15. Look at the stool, the table, and the bookshelf.
The bookshelf is the _____ thing.
The stool is _____ than the table.

16. The vase is the _____ thing in the room.

17. The string from the light is _____ than the pole
of the fan.

© Marshall Cavendish International (Singapore) Private Limited.

Put On Your Thinking Cap!

Challenging Practice

Solve.

Mae moves the counters on a board.
The arrows show the moves.

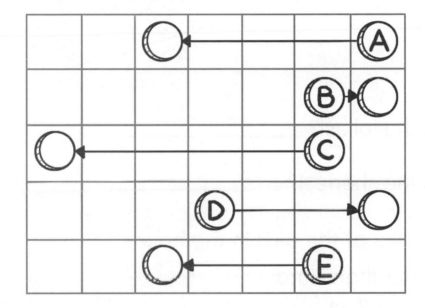

1. Which counter makes the longest move?

    _____

2. Which counter makes the shortest move?

    _____

3. Which counter moves 5 squares? _____

4. Which counters move the same length?

    _____ and _____.

© Marshall Cavendish International (Singapore) Private Limited.

Three boys are lying on a mat.

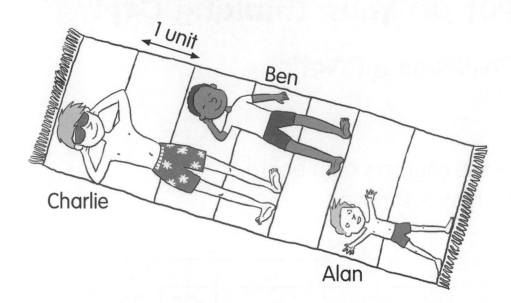

5. Who is the tallest? _____

6. Who is the shortest? _____

Write the names of the girls in the boxes.

7. Tia is taller than Nora.
Sue is the tallest.

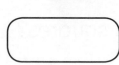

© Marshall Cavendish International (Singapore) Private Limited.

© Marshall Cavendish International (Singapore) Private Limited.

Name: _____ **Date:** _____

Look at the picture and read.
Then draw.

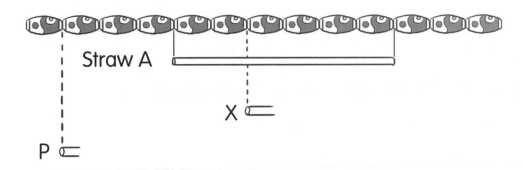

stands for 1 unit.

Straw A

X

P

8. Draw a straw as long as Straw A.
   Start at P.

9. Draw a straw longer than Straw A.
   Start at X.

Arrange the bears in order.
Write the letter.

10.

A   B   C

D

_____ _____ _____ _____

tallest

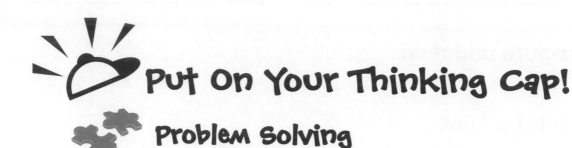

Put On Your Thinking Cap!

Problem Solving

Fill in the blanks.

1. Tim, Ella, Rosa, and Ling knit some scarves.
    Who does each scarf belong to?

    Scarf A   _____

    Scarf B   _____

    Scarf C   _____

    Scarf D   _____

© Marshall Cavendish International (Singapore) Private Limited.

Chapter Review/Test

Vocabulary

Match.

1.   short •

        tall •

        short •

        long •

Write *longest* or *shortest*.

2.

pencil

ruler

paper clip

The paper clip is the _____.

The ruler is the _____.

© Marshall Cavendish International (Singapore) Private Limited.

Concepts and Skills

Draw a start line.
Read and color.

3.   Color the longest ribbon yellow.
      Color the shortest ribbon blue.

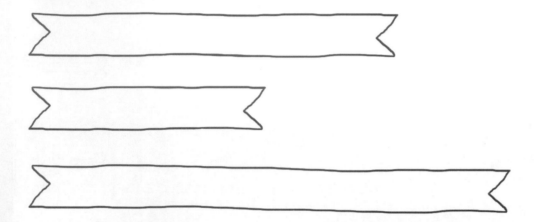

Fill in the blanks.

4.

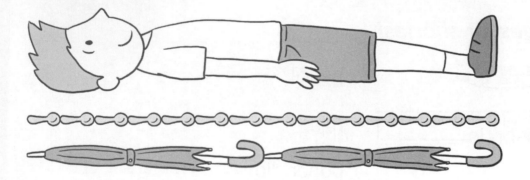

The boy is about _____ ⟿ long.

This is _____ ten and _____ ones.

He is about _____ 🌂 long.

© Marshall Cavendish International (Singapore) Private Limited.

Problem Solving

Solve.

1 ☐ stands for 1 unit.

Madison   Jimar   Patch

5.   Madison is _____ units tall.

6.   Patch is _____ units tall and _____ units long.

7.   The longest balloon is _____ units long.

8.   Whose balloon has the longest string? _____

© Marshall Cavendish International (Singapore) Private Limited.

Solve.

9.   Three children are on stage.
     Ben is taller than Ally.
     Charlie is shorter than Ben.
     Ally is the shortest.

     Who is the tallest?

     _____ is the tallest.

     Who is not the shortest and not the tallest?

     _____

You may draw a picture to help you

© Marshall Cavendish International (Singapore) Private Limited.

Cumulative Review

for Chapters 7 to 9

Concepts and Skills

Circle the ten.
Then fill in the blanks.

1.

Ten and _____ make _____.

10 + ⬜ = ⬜

2.

Ten and _____ make _____.

10 + ⬜ = ⬜

© Marshall Cavendish International (Singapore) Private Limited.

Show the number.

Draw ☐ **for tens and** ☐ **for ones.**

3.

Tens	Ones

10

4.

Tens	Ones

18

Write the number.

Then fill in the blanks.

5.

Set A: _____   Set B: _____

Set _____ has _____ more teddy bears than

Set _____.

Compare.

Fill in the blanks.

6.

| 16 | 19 | 11 | 17 |

_____ is the least number.

_____ is the greatest number.

© Marshall Cavendish International (Singapore) Private Limited.

Complete each number pattern.

7. 9, 10, _____, 12, 13, _____, 15

8. 20, _____, 18, 17, _____, _____, 14, 13

Order the numbers from least to greatest.

9.
| 12 | 17 | 16 | 8 | 11 |

_____ _____ _____ _____ _____

Make a 10.
Then add.

10. 9 + 8 = _____   9 + _____ = 10

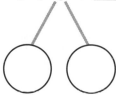

10 + _____ = _____

Group into a 10 and ones.
Then solve.

11. 7 + 13 = _____   **12.** 15 – 8 = _____

Complete.

13. 7 + 7 = _____   **14.** 7 + 8 = _____

15. 16 – 8 = _____   **16.** 12 – _____ = 6

© Marshall Cavendish International (Singapore) Private Limited.

Fill in the blanks.
Use the words in the box.

Trey

Rosa

Lauren

| shorter | shortest | longer | longest | taller | tallest |

17. Rosa is _____ than Lauren.

18. Lauren is _____ than Rosa.

19. Trey is _____ than Rosa and Lauren.

So, Trey is the _____.

20. The tail on the white dog is _____ than the tail on the spotted dog.

21. The tail on the black dog is _____ than the tail on the white dog.

22. The tail on the spotted dog is the _____.

© Marshall Cavendish International (Singapore) Private Limited.

© Marshall Cavendish International (Singapore) Private Limited.

Name: _____   **Date:** _____

Complete.

23.   Draw a start line.

Then draw a strip that is longer than A and shorter than B.

A

B

Fill in the blanks.

24.

The dog collar is about _____ long.

It is about _____ 🦴 long.

25.   1 🪵 stands for 1 unit.

The leash is about _____ units long.

_____ is 10 and _____ units.

Problem Solving

Solve.

26. Grandma bakes 20 muffins.
She gives 8 muffins to Emily.
How many muffins does
Grandma have left?

Grandma has _____ muffins left.

27. 17 insects are in the garden.
9 are bees.
The rest are ladybugs.
How many are ladybugs?

_____ are ladybugs.

© Marshall Cavendish International (Singapore) Private Limited.

Mid-Year Review

Test Prep

Multiple Choice

Fill in the circle next to the correct answer.

1. How many stars are there?

   Ⓐ 10   Ⓑ 8   Ⓒ 7   Ⓓ 6

2. Which number is greater than 8?

   Ⓐ 8   Ⓑ 10   Ⓒ 7   Ⓓ 0

3. Which star makes 10?

   6 + 4   7 + 2   5 + 3   0 + 1

   Ⓐ   Ⓑ   Ⓒ   Ⓓ

© Marshall Cavendish International (Singapore) Private Limited.

4. Which star makes 1 less than 7?

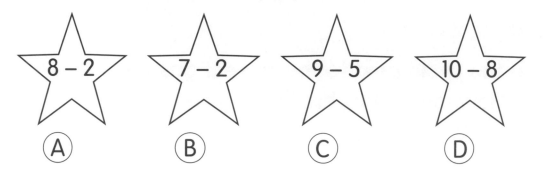

    (A)   (B)   (C)   (D)

5. Find the missing number.

$$\boxed{} + 9 = 10$$

(A) 11   (B) 8   (C) 1   (D) 0

6. Find the missing number.

$$8 - \boxed{} = 4$$

(A) 8   (B) 5   (C) 4   (D) 2

7. How many sides does a ◺ have?

(A) 4   (B) 3   (C) 2   (D) 0

8. How many corners does a ◯ have?

(A) 0   (B) 1   (C) 2   (D) 5

© Marshall Cavendish International (Singapore) Private Limited.

9.   How are these shapes sorted?

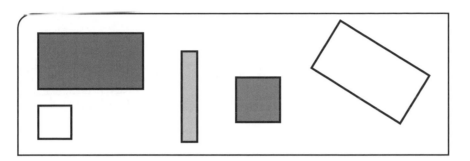

Ⓐ shape

Ⓑ color

Ⓒ size

Ⓓ number of sides

10.   Which solid shape can you roll <u>and</u> slide?

Ⓐ sphere   Ⓑ cone   Ⓒ cube   Ⓓ pyramid

11.   Complete the pattern.

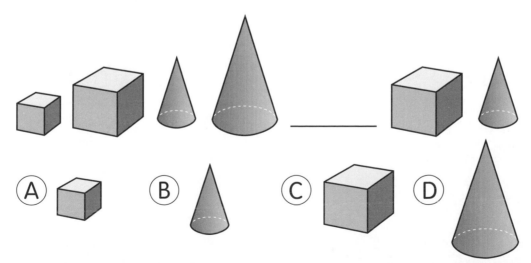

© Marshall Cavendish International (Singapore) Private Limited.

12. In which position is the black bird?

    (A) 3rd   (B) 5th   (C) 9th   (D) 10th

13. What do ten and nine make?

    (A) 1   (B) 9   (C) 19   (D) 20

14. $16 - 8 = ?$

    (A) 8   (B) 9   (C) 16   (D) 18

15. The tennis racket is about _____ shoes long.

    (A) 5   (B) 4   (C) 3   (D) 1

© Marshall Cavendish International (Singapore) Private Limited.

Short Answer

Read the questions carefully.
Write your answers in the space given.

Write the numbers in words.

16.   8   _____

17.   19   _____

18.   12   _____

Complete the number patterns.

19.   _____ 1, 2, 3, _____, 5

20.   _____, 16, 14, _____, 10, 8 _____

Add.

21.   7 + 8 = _____

22.   20 − 7 = _____

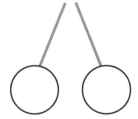   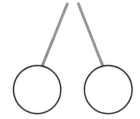

© Marshall Cavendish International (Singapore) Private Limited.

Order the numbers from greatest to least.

23.

| 19 | 9 | 20 | 10 |

_____ _____ _____ _____

Look at the picture.
Circle the words for the shapes you see.

24.

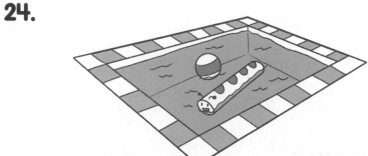

| circle | rectangle | square | triangle |

| sphere | pyramid | cylinder | cone | cube |

© Marshall Cavendish International (Singapore) Private Limited.

Look at the picture.
Then fill in the blanks.
Use the words in the box.

Maria Josh Liping Jamal

left	right
between	above
below	next to
first	second
third	fourth

25. Maria is last from the _____.

26. Jamal is _____ on the right.

27. Liping is _____ Josh and Jamal.

28. The mouse is _____ Josh.

Look at the picture.
Then fill in the blanks.

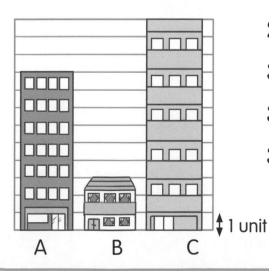

↕ 1 unit

A   B   C

29. Building A is _____ units tall.

30. Building B is _____ units tall.

31. Building C is _____ units tall.

32. Building _____ is the tallest.

© Marshall Cavendish International (Singapore) Private Limited.

Extended Response

Solve.

33.

There are _____ butterflies.

There are _____ spiders.

       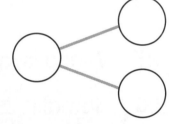

There are _____ butterflies and spiders in all.

34.

There are 8 girls.

2 girls have curly hair.

       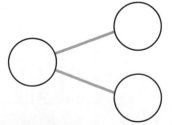

_____ girls have straight hair.

© Marshall Cavendish International (Singapore) Private Limited.

Show the number.

Draw ▯ **for tens and** □ **for ones.**

Then fill in the blanks.

35.

Tens	Ones

17

Tens	Ones

11

_____ is the greater number.

It is greater by _____.

Fill in the blanks.

36. $7 + 8 = ?$ $7 + 8$ is double _____ plus _____.

$7 + 8 = 7 +$ _____ plus _____

$=$ _____ $+ 1$

$=$ _____

© Marshall Cavendish International (Singapore) Private Limited.

37. Mom has 13 buttons.
She uses some to sew a dress.
7 buttons are left.
How many buttons does Mom use?

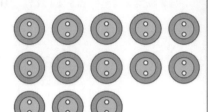

Mom uses _____ buttons.

38. Andrew gives away 9 muffins.
He has 8 muffins left.
How many muffins did he
have at first?

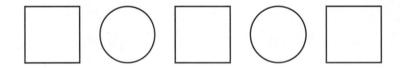

Andrew had _____ muffins at first.

© Marshall Cavendish International (Singapore) Private Limited.

39. Follow the directions:
First, draw a start line.
Next, draw a shorter arrow.
Then, draw an arrow that is longer than the other arrows.
Last, circle the shortest arrow.

© Marshall Cavendish International (Singapore) Private Limited.

BLANK